D0116122

The Love of
America

The Love of
America

Edmund Blair Bolles

Contents

endpapers: the Genesee River gorge, Letchworth State Park, New York

page 1: the Great Cypress Swamp, Florida

pages 2-3: the midtown Manhattan skyline

First published 1979 by
Octopus Books Limited
59 Grosvenor Street, London W1

ISBN 0 7064 0958 2

©1979 Octopus Books Limited

Produced by Mandarin Publishers Limited
22a Westlands Road, Quarry Bay, Hong Kong
Printed in Hong Kong

Foreword

A not infrequent daydream of mine places me in the shoes of my Cronkite (or Krankheydt) ancestors as, among the first New Amsterdam colonists, they sailed into the mouth of the Hudson River and, eventually, beyond. Coming from the low flat lands of their polders, how magnificent that most glorious of river valleys and its border of forested hills must have appeared to them!

There were similar shocks of grandeur awaiting others of our pioneers as they reached the peak of the Appalachians and gazed across the rolling hills beyond; as they crossed the Missouri and from the occasional hillock surveyed a seemingly endless plain; as (and this with some trepidation) they watched the incredible wall of the Rockies rise out of the horizon ahead; as they gazed down on the beauty of San Francisco Bay and Puget Sound.

The pristine glory of those sights, of course, is gone. Civilization has now marked them all; some would say marred them all. Yet there is a grandeur, too, in what man has built, and despite the frequent complaints of homogeneity in the American scene, there are breathtaking vistas still for the discerning eye and the romantic soul.

Some are still of the natural variety, of course—the Berkshires, the Appalachians, the Rockies, Yosemite, Niagara Falls, the Grand Canyon, and the awesome sweep of the Mojave Desert.

But man's implantations also can send a thrill tingling up the spine. There are few experiences that equal the first aerial view of Manhattan on a day when the northwest wind has blown away the haze, the hundreds of skyscrapers reach into the clear blue above and the rivers that surround the island reflect the sun with a billion facets.

New York should be seen first like that, from the air, and so should Los Angeles at night, the fairyland of lights spreading from the base of the mountains to the sea.

Some of man's wonders should be, but seldom are these days, seen first from the land. Houston is an unforgettable mirage, seen that way, rising suddenly as it does out of the singularly unattractive billiard table that is the alluvial plain on which this metropolis grew.

San Francisco's wonder is best seen from Sausalito across the water and one knows why columnist Herb Caen gave it the name that has stuck: 'Baghdad on the Bay.'

Nor is there anything mundane in the view of America at work. From Pittsburgh's Mount Washington, one watches the nation's muscles ripple—by night the flash of the steel mill fires along the banks of the Monongahela and Allegheny; by day the endless thread of trucks and trains and barges against the picket fence of belching smokestacks.

These are some of the special splendors of America. But they are laid against the mosaic that *is* America; the thousands of seaside villages, crossroads towns and cities of superficial sameness but each with a character, and a history, of its own.

The country is vast, the terrain diverse, the people disparate, and yet they form a nation of remarkable unity. In this handsome volume America sits for a portrait that in its presentation is as fascinating as the story it has to tell.

*left: Hyde Street Pier,
San Francisco, with Alcatraz
Island in the background*

C A N A [D A]

Olympic ✱
● Seattle
WASHINGTON
Mt. Rainier ✱
Portland ●
Columbia

OREGON
Crater Lake
Mt. Shasta ▲

RANGE
ROCKY
✱ Glacier
M O N T A N A
Missouri
● Butte
● Helena
Yellowstone

IDAHO
● Boise

NORTH
D A K O T A
● Bismarck

SOUTH
DAKOTA
● Pierre

✱ Yellowstone
✱ Grand Teton
Black Hills

WYOMING
● Cheyenne

NEBRA[SKA]

C A L I F O R N I A
SIERRA
NEVADA
Death Valley

N E V A D A
● Reno
Sacramento ●
San Francisco ●

✱ Yosemite

Las Vegas ●
Hoover Dam

Los Angeles ●

U T A H
● Salt Lake
City

Colorado

✱ Rocky Mountains
● Denver
● Aspen
C O L O R A D O

KAN[SAS]

PACIFIC
OCEAN

✱ Grand Canyon
Grand
Canyon
✱ Painted Desert

✱ Mesa Verde

Rio Grande
● Santa Fe

Petrified Forest ✱
A R I Z O N A
● Phoenix

N E W
M E X I C O
● Albuquerque

OK[LAHOMA]

● Tucson

Fort Wor[th]

Big Bend
✱

T E [X A S]

Rio Grande

M E X I C O

Barrow ●

CANADA

A L A S K A
Nome ●
Yukon
Mt. McKinley ▲

● Anchorage

Sitka ●
Ketchikan ●

0   300 miles
200 400 km

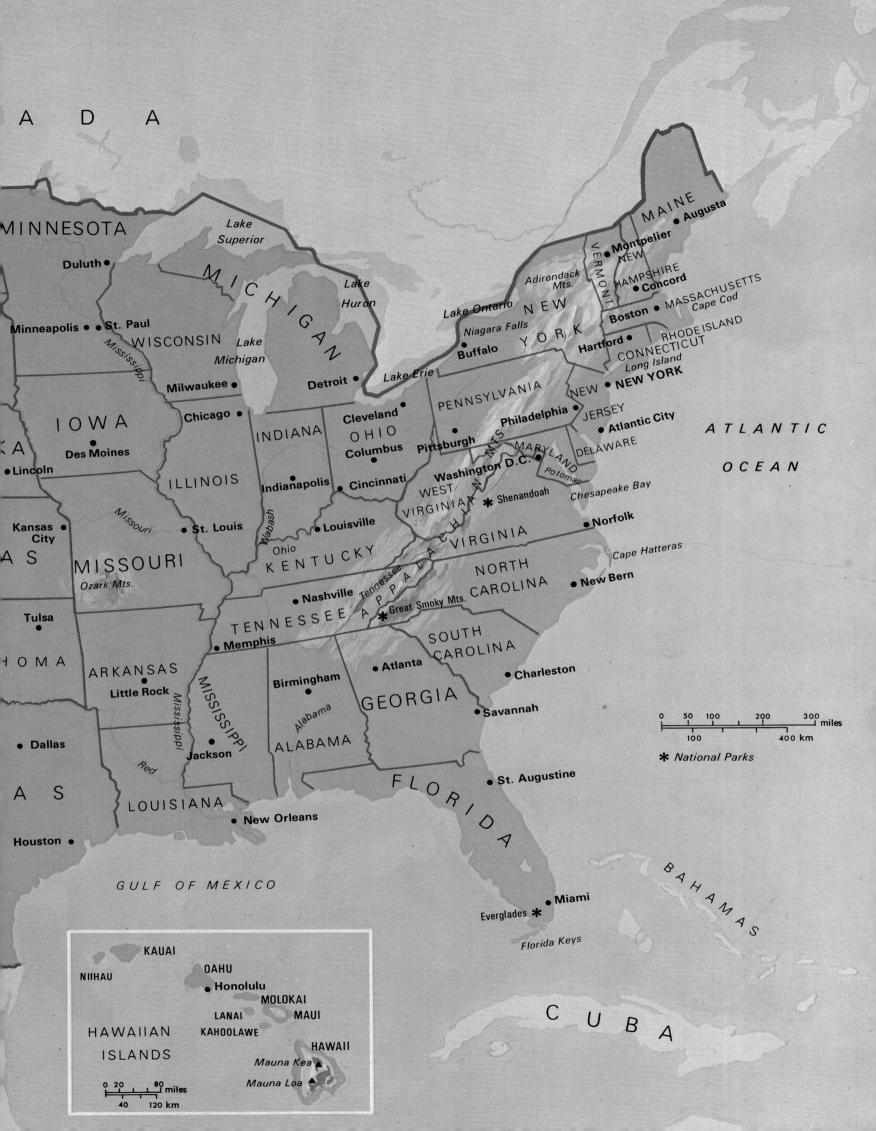

CAN**ADA**

MINNESOTA

Lake
Superior

Duluth •

*Lake
Huron*

MICHIGAN

Minneapolis • • St. Paul

WISCONSIN

*Lake
Michigan*

Milwaukee •

Chicago •

IOWA

Detroit •

Lake Erie

Des Moines •

• Lincoln

ILLINOIS

INDIANA

OHIO

Cleveland •

Columbus
•

Indianapolis •

Cincinnati •

*Adirondack
Mts.*

MAINE

• Augusta

Montpelier •

VERMONT

NEW
HAMPSHIRE

• **Concord**

Lake Ontario

NEW
YORK

Niagara Falls

Buffalo •

Boston • MASSACHUSETTS
Cape Cod

Hartford • RHODE ISLAND

CONNECTICUT

Long Island

PENNSYLVANIA

NEW
JERSEY

• **NEW YORK**

Pittsburgh •

Philadelphia •

• Atlantic City

MARYLAND

DELAWARE

ATLANTIC

OCEAN

Mississippi

Kansas •
City

Missouri

• St. Louis

MISSOURI

Ozark Mts.

Tulsa •

OMA

Little Rock •

ARKANSAS

Wabash

• Louisville

Ohio

KENTUCKY

Washington D.C. •

WEST
VIRGINIA

✱ Shenandoah

Potomac

Chesapeake Bay

VIRGINIA

• Norfolk

Cape Hatteras

NORTH
CAROLINA

• New Bern

APPALACHIAN MTS.

• Nashville

Tennessee

✱ Great Smoky Mts.

TENNESSEE

• Memphis

Mississippi

MISSISSIPPI

Dallas •

Red

Jackson •

Alabama

Birmingham •

• Atlanta

SOUTH
CAROLINA

• Charleston

GEORGIA

• Savannah

ALABAMA

AS

LOUISIANA

• New Orleans

Houston •

FLORIDA

• St. Augustine

0   50 100   200   300
|—|—|————|—————————| miles
    100   400 km

✱ *National Parks*

GULF OF MEXICO

BAHAMAS

Miami
Everglades ✱ •

Florida Keys

CUBA

KAUAI

NIIHAU

OAHU

• Honolulu

MOLOKAI

LANAI   MAUI

KAHOOLAWE

HAWAIIAN

ISLANDS

HAWAII

Mauna Kea ▲

Mauna Loa ▲

0 20   80
|—|——|—————| miles
  40   120 km

The Continent-Wide Nation

Midway through the reign of Queen Elizabeth I, British adventurers began probing into the New World. By then Columbus's voyages were more than three-quarters of a century old and all of South America had been taken, but in the north there was still a giant unknown land. Early British visits there were tentative and brief. In 1579 Francis Drake sailed into a small harbor north of San Francisco Bay, but he soon departed, never to return. A few years later, in 1584, Sir Walter Raleigh made his first try at establishing an American colony, at Roanoke. The effort failed. At that time there seemed no reason to link these two incidents since they occurred at sites as widely separate as Europe's Atlantic seaboard and the far shore of the Caspian Sea. Yet today Roanoke, Drake's Bay, and all the land between has become part of the United States. What was once a continent is now a nation.

This process of unification is at the heart of American history, although for a long time it was far from anyone's mind. Even one and a half centuries after Drake and Raleigh the English settlements in North America extended no more than a few hundred miles inland from the Atlantic coast, and those small colonies saw themselves more as rivals than as part of an American whole.

Occasionally large parts of the present United States had been organized and united by the Indians; some such attempts were even witnessed by the European newcomers. In the east, the Iroquois formed a political confederation of tribes, while at the headwaters of the Mississippi the French explorers encountered a religious movement whose chief symbol was the calumet or 'peace pipe' and which called for peace and unity among neighbors. But neighbors always had more neighbors, and as these movements expanded into new cultures and terrains their capacity for unity, be it religious or political, faded and then died.

It was the Spanish who made the first deliberate attempt to establish a North American empire. Within 50 years of Columbus' first voyage the Spanish managed to locate and plunder all the great civilizations in the New World. By chance, this scooping up of the loose wealth kept Spanish eyes focused first on South and Central America. By the time attention could be brought further north, something had happened to Spain. It is hard to define, but during the late 16th century there was a shift in European strength: power and vitality moved from the Mediterranean to the north. England, France, and the Netherlands were the new centers of action. The Spanish empire grew only a little more, then went into a long stagnation, and ultimately fell apart.

So it was the late-starters, the English settlements, that expanded across the entire North American continent. It required the combined energies of a political and an industrial revolution to do it, but after two centuries of living on no more than a coastal sliver the Americans suddenly seized and conquered the rest of the land.

Left: The Teton Range of the Rocky Mountains stands like a sheer wall towering 7,000 ft (2,100 m) above the floor of the fertile Jackson Hole, Wyoming. Both the prairie and the mountains are now part of Grand Teton National Park. Like so much of America, the first whites to explore the area and learn its paths were fur traders. They gave the mountains their name, 'les trois tetons' (the three breasts). The tallest of the group, Grand Teton, stands 13,747 ft (4,190 m) high.

Below: In the Devils
Postpile National
Monument, California, great
columns of basaltic rock
stand 60 ft (18 m) high.
The wall was formed by
volcanic lava which cracked
as it cooled.

Right: The harbor of
Friendship, Maine is on
Mascongus Bay, one of the
many coves along this
rough portion of the
Atlantic coast. French
fishermen were visiting this
area on a regular basis by
the year 1500. Some
scholars even argue that the
French were fishing in the
cold Maine waters before
Columbus made his first
voyage to America. The bay
is now very popular for
sailing trips.

The stage which Americans hurled themselves upon was not always an easy one to cross. Both the western and eastern edges of the present United States boast mountain ranges. The eastern range, known generally as the Appalachians, is by far the more gentle one, so low that westerners laugh contemptuously at the idea that they are mountains at all. They comprise a long low wall, generally rising only about 3,000 ft (900 m). The tallest peak is Mt Mitchell in North Carolina, a mere 6,684 ft (2,037 m). But what the Appalachians lack in altitude they recover in age, for they are among the oldest mountains in the world. Portions are perhaps a billion years old, making them much older than even the Atlantic Ocean. Geologists now believe that before the Atlantic was born, both Europe and North America were part of a single landmass and that in those days the Appalachians of North America, the Highlands of present-day Scotland and the mountains of Scandinavia, which are all approximately the same age, were part of a continuous chain of wild and rugged peaks.

America's taller and younger west-coast mountains seem to stretch without end. Most easterners tend to call the entire system by the name of the easternmost range, the Rockies, but this practice obscures the vastness of the mountainous area. From Denver, Colorado to Cape Mendocino, California, a distance of over 1,000 miles (1,600 km), the western third of the country is a buckled land. The tallest mountain there is Mt Whitney, 14,494 ft (4,418 m), in the Sierra of California. The view at the summit shows valleys and mountains. Valleys and more mountains can be seen beyond those first ones, and over those further mountains, standing as a hazy line, there are more mountains still.

Between the western and eastern mountain systems is a wide flatland. The territory running from western Pennsylvania to the Rockies, the equivalent of the distance from London to Leningrad, is, with little exception, an enormous plateau. Part of the reason for the sudden and rapid expansion of the United States during the 19th century was that once Americans had managed to cross the Appalachians there seemed to be almost no physical barriers to the occupation of the remaining land. It was during the settlement of the plateau that Americans first began to imagine seriously that it was their 'manifest destiny' to reach all the way across the continent to the Pacific coast.

By spreading over the whole continent America became a nation of contrasts. Its people, land, and history are united but not standardized. Americans value change and variety more than most societies, and, as the rest of this book will show, when Americans talk of their nation's beauty, they have its diversity in mind. Even in the age of jet transport and telecommunications, America is still a giant swatch of land, a place where scenic splendor can be either a painted desert or a giant waterfall, mountain peaks or a smooth prairie that runs to all horizons.

Right: The 3 mile (5 km) wide Mendenhall Glacier is one of the great sights for travelers along the Inland Passage, a 1,000 mile (1,600 km) protected water route which extends from Seattle, Washington to Skagway, Alaska. Mendenhall's 200 ft (60 m) high face drops into the Lynn Canal, the northernmost fjord to penetrate Alaska's coastal range. The glacier lies about midway between Juneau and Skagway.

The South

The South

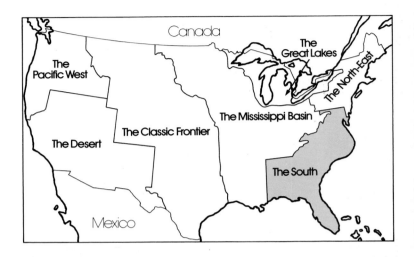

Previous pages: The look of the Old South is honored and made heroic in the design of the Jefferson Memorial. This circular colonnaded structure reflects the tastes of Thomas Jefferson, America's third President, and of many other owners of great plantations. The building, in Washington, D.C., was dedicated on 13 April 1943, the 200th anniversary of Jefferson's birth. The cherry trees which surround the city's Tidal Basin were a gift of the Japanese in 1912. They blossom every April and give the memorial its loveliest setting.

Left: The Hyatt Regency Hotel of Atlanta, Georgia is here reflected in the mirror facade of the Peachtree Center. The dome contains a revolving restaurant.

Above: A log farmhouse up in the Great Smoky Mountains looks much like the homes of the south's pioneer settlers.

The Corsica River is an inlet on the eastern shore of the Chesapeake Bay. Along its short course – less than 10 miles (16 km) – the river passes medium-sized farms, swimming piers where children like to splash, and then halts beneath a bluff at the small town of Centreville. Up on the farms there are people who love horses and who know the story of Centreville and the surrounding Queen Anne's County back to the time of its founding. The setting is the very image of the rural south with its lazy good times and its sense of local tradition.

It is different down by the bay's mouth, at Norfolk, Virginia. Along with its neighbors at Virginia Beach, Newport News, and Portsmouth, Norfolk is a metropolis of over a million people. The navy's Atlantic fleet is based there and lucky visitors can see giant aircraft carriers in the harbor or, even better, watch one pulling out into the bay on its way for an ocean voyage. Norfolk is part of an urban sprawl based on a convenient harbor, military strategy, and increasing industri-

alization. It is quite unlike Centreville, but it too is part of the image of the south, or the New South as publicists like the call it in order to insist on the break with the old rural way of life.

Then, out on the Chesapeake Bay itself are fishing boats, freighters, and tens of thousands of pleasure craft. During a summer weekend the bay fills with about 100,000 private boats as people take a break from their routine to enjoy the comforts of what many still call the 'good life.' Such leisure-time ease is another image of the south, both traditional and modern, and it draws many visitors who want to enjoy the warm weather and slow-moving pace of life.

This mix of tradition, urban growth, and soft comfort is the south that is most accessible to visitors. Naturally the emphasis shifts from place to place, but the blending of these strands is almost always present. Atlanta, Georgia is bustling and booming, unabashedly tied to the here and now, but Civil War sites and souvenirs are still at hand and still draw plenty

Left: Before giant resort hotels could line Miami Beach, the island itself had to be created by dredging.

Below: Cape Canaveral was an unoccupied place of sand dunes until 1950 when it

became the launch site for America's rocket program. The rocket exhibit is now a major attraction.

Bottom: The Florida Keys are connected by the world's longest overwater road. The

Overseas Highway includes 42 bridges, the longest spanning 7 miles (11 km). The Keys themselves are coral islands strung along a 150 mile (240 km) arc extending south-westwards from the tip of Florida.

of visitors. Florida's beaches, retirement villages, and theme parks make it seem like the leisure-time capital of the modern world, but it too has roots in the old south. Indeed Florida contains the famous Suwannee River, which was turned into a symbol of the Old South in a famous minstrel song written by Stephen Foster.

The land itself is not immense, but it is large enough to divide into three distinct categories: tidewater, piedmont and Appalachia. The northern boundary is the famous Mason-Dixon line, the border between Maryland and Pennsylvania. This line is an arbitrary surveyor's mark which begins near tidewater and reaches deep into Appalachia, but it became the point of a great cultural division and even before the Revolution it was seen as the border between north and south.

The tidewater region was the first to be settled. It is the area of coasts, bay shores, and rivers where the ships from England could reach. The oldest southern cities – Charleston, Washington, Williamsburg, and Annapolis – are all in the tidewater.

Appalachia is the western wall. Settlement of its glens and hills was still continuing during the first part of this century. It has the wildest natural scenery in the south. The best way to see it is to do as the mountain men of old and go on foot. A 2,028 mile (3,263 km) trail leads along the mountain-tops from Georgia to Maine, and every year a few hearty souls do make the trip. Many thousands more hike along some part of it.

If that sort of exercise sounds too strenuous, much of it can now be driven. West of Washington, D.C. is the Shenandoah

Above: The courthouse in St Augustine, Florida presides over the oldest city in the United States. St Augustine was founded by the Spanish in 1566.

Right: Mickey Mouse leads a parade through Walt Disney World near Orlando in central Florida.

Far right: The southern tip of Florida is covered by the Everglades swamp. Alligators (which, unlike crocodiles, sometimes live outside the tropics) are its most famous inhabitants. Here the sharp-toothed saw grass grows to 10 or 15 ft (3–5 m). The Everglades National Park covers a little over 2,000 sq miles (5,200 sq km).

National Park, an area once surveyed by George Washington. The park's main road, the Skyline Drive, runs along the top of the mountain ridges and offers excellent views of the Shenandoah Valley below. The gentle river in the middle of the green valley is always a lovely sight. This area saw terrible and endless struggles during the Civil War as the opposing armies pushed each other up and down the valley; the town of Winchester changed hands 76 times.

Beyond the Shenandoah National Park the road is called the Blue Ridge Parkway. It provides what must be the most scenic drive that can be taken through the south. It passes near Virginia's Natural Bridge, a marvel of rock erosion, and then goes on by North Carolina's Mt Mitchell, the tallest mountain in the eastern United States. There are also many possible side trips that can be taken from the parkway. The most important is to Monticello, home of Thomas Jefferson. Jefferson loved to tinker and invent, so his home mixes practical, eccentric, and clever ideas.

At the far end of the parkway are the Great Smoky Mountains, the best place to get a real sense of how wild the Appalachians once were. The name Great Smoky refers to the blue haze that gives the effect of smoke rising on distant ridges. The main ridge-line marks the boundary between North Carolina and Tennessee. For 36 miles (58 km) this line never drops below 5,000 ft (1,500 m) and 16 peaks rise above

6,000 ft (1,800 m). The Smokies are now in America's most heavily visited national park, but a little hiking soon leaves most of the tourists far behind. The Appalachian Trail crosses the ridges of the park and people who walk along the Great Smokies portion may find black bears, white-tailed deer, or even wild turkey. Come in late June when the flame azaleas are in blossom. That is wild America at its loveliest.

Of course the view from the base of the mountains looking up is a good one too. This piedmont district is the area closest to the old southern stereotype. It is rural, still rather impoverished, and fiercely proud of its local history. The major crops are tobacco and cotton, but industrialization is proceeding rapidly in certain areas, particularly near important highways as a drive along US Highway 1 from Richmond, Virginia to Augusta, Georgia demonstrates. One of the most rapidly growing parts of this region is the Raleigh-Durham area of North Carolina; however, in both North and South Carolinas the majority of the population is still rural.

The capital of the piedmont is Atlanta, Georgia, the city which has made itself the symbol of the modern south. Atlanta is industrial: there are over 1,500 manufacturing plants in the area. It is cosmopolitan, conducting international and national business and serving as a popular convention center. It is a major distribution point for markets throughout the south. Atlanta was also the first important southern city to

21

The South

Below: The restorations at Williamsburg show how the houses, main streets, and transport appeared during the colonial era. The town was designated Virginia's capital in 1699 and prospered for the next 80 years, until Richmond became the capital. Many of Virginia's decisions leading to the break with Britain were made at Williamsburg. Traditional crafts such as wigmaking and shoemaking are still continued here.

elect a black mayor; it was the birthplace of Martin Luther King Jr, the assassinated black civil rights leader, and plans are under way to construct a memorial to King. Such developments testify to a serious change in southern values and in the distribution of political power.

Atlanta too is proud of its history, particularly the fact that it is a phoenix which literally rose from its ashes despite the worst that the Northern army could do to it. On 15 November 1864, when the city was less than 30 years old, it was deliberately burned to the ground. 'Gate City of the South, farewell,' a Union soldier wrote after watching the fire, but a new city arose at once. Sites of the long siege of Atlanta which preceded its burning are still popular visitor attractions.

There are not many other Civil War sites in the piedmont; most of the war was fought on the edges of the south. Apart from the invasion of the Georgia heartland, the only other penetration of the piedmont was the invasion that finally ended the war. This conclusive campaign was fought in Virginia, beginning with the Battle of the Wilderness in May 1864. General Grant then began a long and terrible hounding of Lee's army. For a while there was stalemated trench warfare, but Lee was eventually forced into further retreat and final surrender at Appomattox on 9 April 1865. All of these battlefields are marked and most are preserved. It is the irony of such sites that they are now almost always peaceful and rather lovely places to visit.

Geologically speaking, the piedmont ends near Atlanta, for there the Appalachians become easier to traverse, permitting more overland travel to the west. In fact it was this important transportation link which led to Atlanta's founding and early growth. But culturally speaking, the piedmont continues both south into Florida and west into Alabama. Alabama in particular feels like the piedmont. Over 40 per cent of its people are country folk. (Only a quarter of the US population as a whole lives in rural areas.) Alabama towns like Dothan which are far from major highways are much like their counterparts in the Carolina and Georgia piedmont or, for that matter, on Maryland's eastern shore.

Florida, too, has more of the piedmont flavor than many people expect. The western panhandle is often said to be 'more like Alabama and Georgia than Florida.' The remark means it is a place where the residents are typically natives of the area and where the towns are not on the main tourist circuits. But even deep in the Florida peninsula we can still find areas that are rural and local. Lake Okeechobee is only a little more than 100 miles (160 km) from the Florida mainland's southern tip and only an hour's drive from the super-luxury resort of Palm Beach, but nobody who drives alongside of it will have much trouble telling he is in the south.

The 'real Florida' so beloved by vacationers and Yankees who no longer wish to put up with snow once seemed like quite a deviation from the rest of the south, but now that other

Below: The Capitol took 70 years to build. George Washington laid the cornerstone in 1793 and the dome was completed during the Civil War, in 1863, after the design had been changed several times.

Below right: The White House has been the official residence of the President since 1800. It was burned by British troops in 1814, but was promptly rebuilt by the original architect, James Hoban.

southern areas are industrializing and building modern cities we can see that modern Florida still carries much of southern tradition with it. Easy comfort and hospitality rather than a puritan scorn of pleasure have always been a part of southern living and have long attracted people.

Florida now gets a lot of immigrants and visitors. Retired people move there to enjoy year-round warmth and leisure. Working people come down for a winter vacation. College students go there during spring vacation. In the summer, families bring their children to the many enormous amusement parks near the city of Orlando. Even the swamps, which once seemed good for little more than draining, are now appreciated. The Everglades of southern Florida draw naturalists and tourists alike to observe the wildlife.

The drive down Florida's east coast reveals how broad the range of attractions for visitors is. St Augustine, in the north, was founded by the Spanish and is the oldest city in the United States. Below that is Daytona Beach, a popular auto-racing site. Then comes Cape Canaveral and the Kennedy space-launch center. Further south is Stuart, reputed to be the sail-fish capital of the Atlantic. The super-resort towns come next: Palm Beach, Pompano Beach, and Miami Beach are one right after another.

In the wake of all this migrant activity, commerce has grown. Florida is now an important cattle-raising state. The city of Miami has become a major shipping point for freight traveling to and from Latin America, while, on Florida's west coast, Tampa is both an important industrial city and a popular resort area.

Before anyone decides that such a mixture of good beaches, history, and tourist appeal is somehow peculiar to Florida, consider the beaches around Nags Head and Cape Hatteras on North Carolina's Outer Banks. The sea is not too suitable for a winter swim, but the beaches are popular summer vacation spots. Visitors soon find that this tiny sliver of land – it is really more sand dune than land – has many interesting sites and stories connected with it. Just above Nags Head is Kitty Hawk, where the Wright brothers flew the first airplane. Right behind Nags Head is Roanoke Island; it was at Roanoke that the English under Sir Walter Raleigh made their first attempts to colonize the New World.

Horrifying stories of the sea tell of the Atlantic side of the Outer Banks. In this area there is a ceaseless tug-of-war between earth and ocean as islands grow, collapse, and change their shape. The most dangerous place is the Diamond Shoals, a 12-mile (19-km) shallows off the point of Cape Hatteras which is littered with shipwrecks. The rough seas move submerged banks so quickly that one day's safe channel through the shoals cannot always be passed the next. In the four centuries since the English came to the New World, hundreds of ships of every size and weight have sunk near Hatteras. It is no wonder, then, that the first efforts to colonize Roanoke were disasters. The wildest, most dangerous shore in the western Atlantic is no place to try to found a settlement which will be dependent on supplies brought from across the sea.

The colonizers were given fair warning. In June of 1585 seven ships carrying the would-be settlers tried to sail through a break in the Outer Banks toward Roanoke. All seven ran aground. They were refloated with the tide, but three days later the group's flagship, *Tiger,* with 160 men aboard, was again grounded and this time the seas were so rough that the ship was in serious danger of breaking up. After heroic efforts on the part of the rest of the fleet the *Tiger* was beached, but the proposed colony's store of corn, salt, meal, rice, and biscuit was soaked in salt water and almost all was spoiled. And still today the beaches are wild and awesome. Late in almost every summer there is a weather report warning that a hurricane with winds of 100 miles (160 km) per hour is 'moving toward Cape Hatteras.'

Only after the English discovered the calmer waters of the Chesapeake Bay were they able to found permanent settlements. The society which appeared in these tidewater areas was similar to the one which expanded into the piedmont, the chief difference perhaps being the tendency of tidewater areas to produce government cities. The most famous of these old tidewater capitals is Williamsburg, Virginia. Williamsburg pretty much went to sleep after 1780, when the capital was moved to Richmond; however, during the past 50 years many of the buildings have been restored or even completely rebuilt. The old state building, for example, was gone, and a carefully researched duplicate has been constructed.

Less artificial is Annapolis. It has been Maryland's capital since 1694 and as far as age and historic importance are concerned it is the equal of Williamsburg, but Annapolis is still the state capital and remains a living, if quiet, city. Its colonial district is the largest in America, 40 square blocks, and contains many fine old houses. In fact Annapolis is reputed to have more Georgian houses than the City of London. One of the best is the home of Samuel Chase, a signatory of the Declaration of Independence and later a justice of the Supreme Court. The present state house dates from 1772 and is the oldest one in the nation which has seen continuous use.

The greatest of these government cities is the national capital, Washington, D.C. (D.C. stands for 'District of Columbia.') At the time of its designation as center for the new federal government, the site was a typical southern tidewater area. The leading citizens of the region were all farmers and even today some old plantation homes have been preserved near Washington. Just across the Potomac River from the Lincoln Memorial is the Custis-Lee Mansion. It was the home of Robert E. Lee, commander of the Confederate Army. George Washington's estate, Mount Vernon, is only a brief drive down the Potomac. During Washington's lifetime the plantation covered 8,000 acres (3,250 hectares). Its chief crops were tobacco and wheat. Around the next bend in the Potomac is another old plantation, Gunston Hall. This spot was the home of George Mason, author of Virginia's Declaration of Rights; that document first shaped Virginia's revolutionary-era constitution and then the Bill of Rights of the US Constitution. Within Washington, D.C. itself, the best reminder of the town's origins is found in the narrow gorge that cuts through much of the city. This area is Rock Creek Park, a long patch of countryside in the middle of town. Towards the northern end of the park, out beyond the zoo, is an old mill, a dam, and a mill pond. Only a short distance away, up at the top of the gorge, is the hurly-burly of 16th Street, but here it is quiet. The mill has been restored to operation and serves as a reminder of the days before the district was selected to become a great city.

Another part of Washington which predates its selection as the national capital is Georgetown. For almost two centuries this section of town has been the residential district for many of the nation's most powerful officers. The rows of fashionable houses on P and Q Streets are popular places for visitors to the city and Georgetown shops are among the smartest in Washington.

From the beginning, however, it has been the success of the federal government which has shaped the growth of Washington, D.C., and the city's chief area of interest has always been around the Mall, a wide lawn connecting the main government buildings. At one end stands the Capitol building, the Su-

Above: Gasoline is only gasoline, but a good firecracker is an explosion. Along South Carolina's coastal highway, US 17, a gas station advertises its wares. Across the state line, in North Carolina, liquor and fireworks cannot be sold.

Right: Lace House in Columbia, South Carolina is across from the Governor's Mansion and is officially part of his residence. It is used to accommodate visiting dignitaries and for formal banquets. Columbia itself was established in 1786 as the state capital and gave South Carolina's inland areas a counterbalance to the growing power of coastal Charleston. Most of the city was destroyed by fire when Union troops entered it in 1865. President Woodrow Wilson's boyhood home here is now a museum.

preme Court, and the Library of Congress. At the other end is the White House and the monuments honoring presidents Washington, Lincoln, and Jefferson. In between are a series of undistinguished federal office buildings and some marvelous museums – the National Gallery of Art and the Smithsonian Institute's many branches. A full tour of the Mall with its glimpses of American history and the workings of politics deserves several days.

This mixture of federal business in a southern setting has always given Washington its own flavor. President Kennedy used to joke that it was 'a city of northern charm and southern efficiency.' The one great and purely southern old city is Charleston in South Carolina. The old south was organized around plantations and did not encourage much urban life, but sometimes a regular city could not be avoided. South Carolina's staple crop was rice, a grain that grew best in malaria-infested areas, and during the summer's mosquito season plantation owners fled their mansions to live in town houses. Charleston thus became the great urban and commercial center of the Old South. Many of those houses remain in use and their gardens are proudly maintained. By a long-standing tradition an open front gate means that a passer-by is welcome to enter and enjoy the beauty of the garden. April is the time of blossom for the south's most famous flowers: magnolia, oleander, hydrangea, and crape myrtle. Charleston's Middleton Place contains America's oldest landscaped gardens. The city is also the home of 'Catfish Row,' the black ghetto made famous in George Gershwin's opera *Porgy and Bess*.

It is the history and culture represented by the gardens and society of Charleston which continue to be the major travel attraction throughout the south. The old south of plantations is gone, but interest in that era survives, and some of the plantation houses can be visited. Since they are out in the country, they are often isolated from other tourist sites, but an important aspect of the southern atmosphere is the way travel throughout the region reveals so many hints of the past. The Biltmore Mansion in Asheville, North Carolina and Oakleigh House in Mobile, Alabama both merit a visit from anyone in the vicinity. In quiet Madison, Georgia there are still a number of well-preserved plantation houses. General Sherman's army was persuaded not to burn them because the local Congressman had opposed the break with the union.

Old courthouses, still in use, are another typical feature of the rural south and create a flavor of stability and tradition not found in many other parts of the country. In Centreville, Maryland the county courthouse dates to the 18th century. Outsiders who maintain that little has happened in the town since the courthouse was built will find that Centreville residents tend to agree, only they boast of the absence of change with the pride of a true country conservative.

The different atmosphere and values that comprise the south long kept the country apart. Well before the Civil War, even before the Revolution, the difference between north and south was apparent to all. As the south expanded across the Appalachians and into the Mississippi basin much of its culture changed, and its difference with the north became more sharply defined in terms of slavery; eventually the tensions erupted into war. The result of that catastrophe was a long stagnation in the south. The region was ignored by the rest of the country; it received almost no immigrants; capital investments in the region were rare.

Today the situation is changing. Urbanization and industrialization are going on throughout the region. The flow of money into a long-impoverished area is important and even exciting, but there is a more important flow under way. For the first time in a century people are moving into many areas of the south. Internal migrations have been the key to the growth and unification of the nation, and now the south, too, is seen as a place of new opportunity. The bitterness of the Civil War lasted for generations, but at last a mutual tolerance and acceptance has appeared on both sides and the old regional suspicions now sound a bit old-fashioned.

The North-East

The North-East

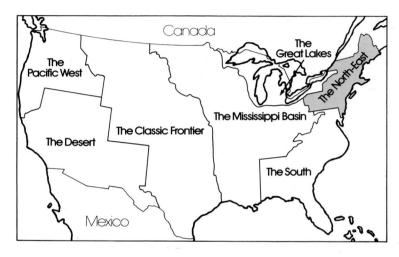

According to the US Bureau of the Census, over 17 million people live in New York City and its enormous suburbs. That figure represents eight per cent of the total American population. No wonder then that when most people think of the north-eastern United States they think first of New York. In its way the city is as wondrous as the Grand Canyon; it is an ultimate in what people have created.

People who love New York talk about its human features—ideas, buildings, crowds, enthusiasm—and a person's response to the city depends on how he feels about people; not people in the abstract, but fleshy people who hope, sweat, fail, think, and do. For a visitor it can all be a bit dismaying. There are so many things that are happening, so much life in the streets, that it is hard to know where to begin. Most end up doing two things. They go shopping and they take advantage of the many available arts.

Performing arts are everywhere. Dramatic theater, ballet, orchestras, two resident opera companies, and movies (old and new) are a part of the city's daily life. Visual arts are also abundant. Anyone interested in the latest ideas about painting or sculpture should go to the SoHo area, below Greenwich Village. It is full of small galleries and visitors are welcome to come and look for free. For those who find the experimental edges of art a little too puzzling the galleries on upper Madison Avenue display the work of more popular artists whose success is able to command higher prices than are typical in SoHo.

Previous pages: Many of the world's most remarkable skyscrapers can be seen by looking north from the top of New York City's Empire State Building. Off to the right, with its back to the East River, is the United Nations Building. The extensive use of glass on its broad face informed the world of the new possibilities in modern construction. A few blocks to the west (left) is the scaled spire of the Chrysler Building, the greatest achievement in the Art Deco style of skyscrapers. The noticeable stepping, or narrowing, of the building as it climbs toward its 77th storey summit was a standard way of preventing the city from becoming a dark canyon with sheer walls and no plays of light. Still further to the left is the 59-storey Pan Am Building. Its broad roof can be used for helicopter landings. North of it stand the corporate headquarters which line Park Avenue, while well to the west is Rockefeller Center. The 66-storey RCA Building is the centerpiece of this 14-building project that covers three city blocks.

Left: Central Park, in the heart of Manhattan Island, is a favorite place of New Yorkers. Summer nights attract thousands who come for free performances of Shakespeare, opera, and the New York Philharmonic Orchestra. Winter draws ice skaters and even a few cross-country skiers. The park was begun in 1857 and was one of the first large parks to be landscaped rather than left in its wild state. Its immediate success brought many more commissions to the principal architect, Frederick Law Olmstead, and the ideas he first put forth in Central Park were repeated in many other parks elsewhere.

Right: Times Square is the center of New York's theater district. Although the neon signs often change, the effect does not. Broadway has been called 'The Great White Way' since the 1890s.

There are also a great many public museums and even exhibits sponsored by business; for example, Kodak offers a continuing series of photography shows and a few blocks away the Burlington Corporation has a display of textiles and patterns.

The city's most sought-after art is its architecture. The United Nations Headquarters, Rockefeller Center, and the Empire State Building are always full of visitors speaking a Babel of languages. To get a full sense of the power of the city's tall buildings every visitor should take two particular walks. The first goes west from Fifth Avenue along 56th Street. When you reach the Avenue of the Americas, turn south, and suddenly the heights of the Rockefeller Center Extension soar above you. By themselves none of these buildings are very distinguished, but together, especially in the light of a sunset,

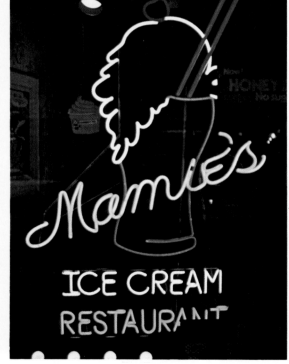

Above: The triumph of steel technology is everywhere represented in lower Manhattan. The giant towers of the financial district are only possible because of steel's ability to *support sheer walls. The Brooklyn Bridge, opened in 1883, was the first suspension bridge to use steel cables. Its completion demonstrated that the engineering problems in* *these enormous spans had at last been resolved.*

Top: Fifth Avenue between 42nd and 59th Streets is remarkable for the density of its pedestrian traffic. *Above left: A New York policeman.*

Above: Neon signs are everywhere — they can look like pen and ink drawings in a New York magazine.

The North-East

Below: Washington Irving's tale 'Rip Van Winkle' begins, 'Whoever has made a voyage up the Hudson must remember the Catskill Mountains. Every change of season, every change of weather, indeed, every hour produces some change in the magical hues and shapes of these mountains.' Although the story was first published 150 years ago, the description is still accurate. The Catskills have changed very little since then.

they form a classic unit, like the columns of a giant temple.

The second walk begins at 50th Street and goes south along Park Avenue. Again the visitor is walking toward enormous buildings that rise up and out of view. Directly ahead, straddling the avenue, is the New York General Building, and behind that is the Pan Am Building. The effect is like being in some enormous box canyon, and at night, when the buildings are lit up, the strength of the scene is religiously humbling.

New York is also full of unknown buildings that catch and please the eye. No guide is necessary to find such structures—just start walking and keep your head up. The section along Broadway between 72nd and 79th Streets, for example, is seldom visited by tourists, yet it is full of grand apartment buildings that date from the turn of the century. The majority of them are still in reasonably good condition. Best of all is the Ansonia at 74th Street. It is a fantasy of wrought-iron balconies, variously shaped windows, and roof turrets. Enrico Caruso used to live there. At the end of this short stroll, beside the subway entrance at 79th Street, is an old Baptist Church erected during the 1890s. It looks straightforward enough until you notice that its two towers are done in completely different styles. In fact, one side has a steeple and one does not. Why? Apparently the architect was a free spirit, the sort of person New York has always loved.

Because of the cultural, commercial, and transportive dominance greater New York has over the region, many out-siders assume the whole north-east has been paved over and turned into one continuous city. A word has been coined, 'megalopolis,' to name specifically the phenomenon. So it comes as a surprise to visitors to find that outside of New York there is still plenty of countryside and even places that could be called wilderness.

Geographically speaking, the north-east is much like the south. Coastal rivers and bays give way to a flatland which halts abruptly at the Appalachian mountains. The mountains come closer to the coast in the north-east, so there is less of the sort of piedmont country which is found in the south.

Also as in the south, the wildest country is in the mountains. The White Mountains of New Hampshire, Pennsylvania's Poconos, New York's Catskills and Adirondacks, and the Green Mountains of Vermont are all in the Appalachian system. So are the Berkshires in Massachusetts and the gentle Litchfield Hills of Connecticut. Some of these mountains have been developed for visitors. Vermont and New Hampshire are favorite ski resorts and the Poconos and Catskills are busy summer places. Still other parts are neither much used nor easy to reach. Stretches of the Adirondack Park in upper New York are still accessible only on foot. The Maine Appalachians are particularly rugged and demanding. At the northern end of the Appalachian Trail, Maine's Mt Katahdin has thousand-foot (300-m) high sheer walls. Its summit reaches 5,267 ft (1,600 m) and offers a view as isolated and wild as any to be

Below: The Adirondack mountains in northern New York State were named for the Indian tribe that once lived in them. According to Samuel de Champlain, the first white explorer in the area, the Indians were 'tree eaters.' Although this report seems doubtful, the Indians would never have gone hungry if it were true. The mountains are now one of America's greatest wildland attractions and still remain unspoiled.

found in the country east of the Rockies.

Below the mountains the country has its heaviest population concentrations, yet this area is also a good one for country drives. Arcing across the whole north-east is a farmland with low hills and plenty of trees. There are good and convenient roads that lead through a charming countryside of small farms and quiet towns. These trails provide the clearest idea of what the original expectations for the north-east were: a settled land where the beauty of nature and design are joined.

North-western New Jersey has many parks and rivers where the fishing is good, and despite the area's proximity to New York City it is neither well known nor served by super-highways. The Hudson River Valley above New York City is also lovely, and people who travel along its eastern bank find that it is reasonably quiet as well. Western Connecticut and Massachusetts offer the almost unknown Housatonic Valley. And of course the states which lie entirely north of Boston—Maine, Vermont, and New Hampshire—are famous for their combination of easy access yet preserved wildness.

Traditionally there are two times when these 'secret' routes are most lovely: during autumn when the leaves turn to red and amber and during the spring when the buds come out. The tradition is a sound one, but the north-eastern farmland has its beauties and permanencies for every season. Low-lying stone walls, old inns which often boast of at least one minor claim to history, smooth rolling hills, and old covered bridges are always there whatever the weather or season may be.

Travelers who are somehow tired of mountains and farmland still do not have to turn to the cities for their entertainment and recreation. There is, after all, the north-east's long coastline. Ocean resorts are stretched along its whole length from Bethany Beach, Delaware to Bar Harbor in Maine. Boating enthusiasts fill Long Island Sound throughout the summer and even landlubbers come to Newport, Rhode Island to watch the world's most famous yacht race, the America's Cup. For those who like the wildest shores there is Maine. There, sandy beaches give way to rocky ones and the water grows much colder, chilled as it is by the Labrador Current. One of the most isolated places to explore on the Maine coast is Manticus Rock, a rugged and desolate island that attracts many bird watchers. It is the only place in the United States where the Atlantic puffin can be found.

The most famous and loveliest of all the coastal resorts is Cape Cod. Every year hundreds of thousands of 'summer people' and weekend visitors flow over the Cape to relax on beaches, eat hamburgers, and snap pictures of the cranberry bog at Dennis or the Pilgrim Monument at Provincetown. The Cape is so attractive that it even draws people who hate crowds. They have two solutions. One is to come in winter when the other visitors are gone, or else they head for the less commonly visited north side of the Cape. Sandy Neck, across from Barnstable, for example, is a wild place of sand dunes

which border on a marsh rich in fish and birdlife. Deer are sometimes seen as well. The best time for a walk is shortly after dawn when the wildlife is active, the heat is not too strong, and the people who drive beach-buggies are still in bed.

Visitors to the coast also find plenty of reminders of the time when much of the north-eastern seaboard was active in fishing and in developing ocean trade. Towns like Bath, Maine and Salem, Massachusetts were once might ports whose names were known around the world. Ships from Bath carried the ice of the Kennebec River to New York, Philadelphia, and even around the tip of South America for sale in the Pacific. Salem ships went east, passed the Cape of Good Hope, traded in Zanzibar, and crossed the Indian Ocean to buy Chinese goods at Canton.

The best opportunity to see what a seaport of those old days looked like is at Mystic, Connecticut. Mystic itself was never much of a port, but the Marine Historical Association has constructed a charming replica of an old waterfront and has brought in a number of fine old sailing vessels to look at. The only surviving American whaling ship, the *Charles W. Morgan*, may be seen in Mystic harbor.

Thanks to Herman Melville's story of *Moby Dick*, whaling is the north-east's most famous sailing tradition. The classic whaling port that still charms every visitor is Nantucket, from which Melville sailed. Even today visitors must spend several hours traveling by ferry from Cape Cod to this island at the edge of the Gulf Stream. The passage increases the sense of moving back into one of the secret places of time. The small gray harbor of wooden houses and weathered sailing vessels convinces the newcomer that Captain Ahab's acquaintances are still nearby.

The impression is increased the more a visitor is familiar with Melville's book. Nantucket family names like Coffin and Starbuck appear in the pages of *Moby Dick* and are still found on the island. A hearty bowl of chowder still leads the menu in almost every restaurant, and Nantucket Island is still so sandy that 'one blade of grass makes an oasis.' Only the whaling is gone.

Nantucket developed the industry, but during the 1840s the lead shifted to New Bedford on the mainland. The railroad had made the islands uncompetitive and suddenly many of the mainland cities turned to whaling. Even Wilmington, Delaware used to send ships from its shore, bound for the Horn and the Pacific whales beyond. But even though the last voyage to begin in Nantucket set sail in 1870, a Nantucket visitor today is likely to start insisting that if he only waits a little while, a whaling ship loaded with sperm oil and tales of the South Sea is sure to sail into the harbor.

Left: Vermont in autumn is a symbol of what many Americans consider their country's basic values. It is rural, containing no cities large enough to be designated by the Census Bureau as metropolitan areas. It is independent; so much so that even in the days of the revolution Vermonters did not want to join the other colonies in the fight against Britain.

Vermont declared itself an independent republic in 1777 and did not join the Union until 1791. The state is also a haven of natural beauty. The dairy farms and towns are scattered down in the valleys, leaving the upland regions to the wildlife. There are still some bears and Vermont's wild deer population is denser than in any other state.

The North-East

The coastal towns and islands point out that the greatest differences between the north-east and the south are cultural and historical. Geographically the major difference between the two regions is probably the climate; the north is colder. However, a strong social difference grew in the two regions. The farms of the north-east tended to be less self-reliant than the great plantations of the south, and farm settlements soon fostered towns where trade and even a little simple industry could develop.

Much of America's politics, commerce, and manufacturing began in this region, and travelers through the north-east continually stumble onto sites where some bit of history was played out. A visitor to Falmouth, Massachusetts may only want to enjoy the beach of Cape Cod, but he soon learns that the village church has a bell cast by Paul Revere, that the old inn was fired on by a British ship during the War of 1812, and that the birthplace of Katherine Lee Bates, author of the song 'America the Beautiful,' is in the town as well.

Elsewhere another person may be reaching Tarrytown, New York, drawn to it because it offers a bridge across the Hudson River. But once there the traveler finds the Sleepy Hollow Restorations. America's first author of note, Washington Irving, lived in Tarrytown for 24 years and his house, Sunnyside, can be visited along with several other 18th century homes in the area.

Or perhaps while driving through southern Pennsylvania a traveler may notice a sign pointing to Gettysburg Battlefield. It was there that the northernmost penetration of Robert E. Lee and the Confederate Army was stopped. The terrain is typical of the land below the mountains, and suddenly the military significance of such country is made clear. Gentle hills become lookout points. Stone fences are transformed into fortified positions.

America's cultural heritage is also the primary attraction of the two other great cities of the north-eastern region, Boston and Philadelphia. Publicists for these two cities have decided that Boston is the 'cradle of liberty' and Philadelphia the 'birthplace of the nation.' It would be hard to maintain such absolutes under cross-examination, but the essential idea is right enough, and parents are correct when they tell their children, 'It was here that much of what America treasures most began.'

Boston is the older city. It was founded in 1630 and immediately began to swell with Puritan refugees fleeing an England on the eve of civil war. To American eyes, at least, the oldest part of Boston seems more European than American. The streets bend and narrow in unexpected ways instead of following the straight lines favored by the real-estate developers and utopian idealists who founded so many other American cities. This disregard of geometry gives the streets of Boston a special interest for the eye, and much of it should be explored slowly, on foot.

Two good walks are on fashionable Beacon Hill and through Harvard University in Cambridge; however, the most popular walking route is along the redbrick path that marks the 'Freedom Trail.' It begins at the Boston Common, a large village green at the foot of Beacon Hill, and leads past many places associated with the Revolution. Some of the sites are quiet places like the Old Corner Bookstore; others like the Old North Church have a simple dignity to them; and still others, such as the sites of the Boston Massacre and the Boston Tea Party, refer to the turmoil of two centuries ago.

Right: The old pier in Provincetown, Massachusetts at the far end of Cape Cod is a familiar sight to the many vacationers who come to the town each summer for the marvelous sailing, fishing, and swimming.

Below: The USS 'Constitution', known as 'Old Ironsides', is still listed as a commissioned ship of the US Navy. It saw action against Tripoli (1801–5) and against the British during the War of 1812. It now sits in Boston Harbor.

Right: Nauset lighthouse is set in the marshes of Cape Cod National Seashore.

Far right: Lobster packers in Portland, Maine prepare the state's most famous seafood for shipment.

Boston was the rabble-rouser of America's drive for independence. It featured scenes of raging mobs in the foreground and Sam Adams quietly organizing in the background. Time after time Boston crowds committed outrages against the established order and, to the consternation of the British, the leading people of the colonies consistently argued that it was more important to preserve American independence than it was to seize control of unruly mobs. A walk along the Freedom Trail leads past sites which must shock and astonish anyone who believes in the primacy of law.

A journey from Boston to nearby Concord brings travelers to the site of the complete collapse of British authority. Concord today seems like a quiet and orderly place. From the looks of it, it is quite in keeping that many of its buildings are associated with a literary past. Ralph Waldo Emerson, Henry David Thoreau, Margaret Fuller, and Louisa May Alcott lived in Concord and wrote their essays in these houses. But it was also in Concord that 'the embattled farmers stood and fired the shot heard round the world.' The Revolutionary War began just outside the town. The battlefield, historic houses of the period, and the graves of unknown British soldiers can all be visited. It seems that the 'cradle of liberty' got a pretty vigorous rocking.

A different atmosphere prevails in Philadelphia. Instead of the random bends found in the streets of old Boston, the oldest part of Philadelphia is squared off as neatly as graph paper. A look at individual old buildings shows the architects had much

in common with those in Boston, but the setting is so tidy that the whole place has a different feel to it. However, Philadelphia is like Boston in that it offers fine museums, handsome old squares, and splendid restaurants, particularly for seafood. Yet it is the association of the city with America's founding that brings the most visitors.

The main historical site is the old Pennsylvania State House, now called Independence Hall. It was there that the Declaration of Independence was approved and signed in July 1776. It was also there that in 1787 the present Constitution of the United States was drafted. The steeple of Independence Hall was the place where one of America's most famous symbols of freedom, the Liberty Bell, was originally hung. The bell was cast in London in 1752 and bears the inscription, 'Proclaim Liberty Throughout All the Land Unto All the Inhabitants Thereof.'

Philadelphia's greatest citizen was Benjamin Franklin, and a pretty good tour of the city can be made just by visiting the sites associated with his life. He signed both the Declaration of Independence and the Constitution, so Independence Hall would be prominent in such a tour. Next to the Hall is the American Philosophical Society building. The organization was founded by Franklin in 1743 and was the first learned society in America. Franklin was also a great financial promoter. The Pennsylvania Hospital, the nation's oldest hospital, was begun by financing which Franklin organized in 1751.

Below: The masterpiece of Beaux-Arts architect Henry Hobson Richardson was Sever Hall. It stands on America's oldest campus: Harvard University, Cambridge, Massachusetts, founded in 1636.

Far left: The home of Louisa May Alcott in Concord, Mass. was known as 'The Wayside.' Emerson and Thoreau were great friends of the Alcotts, and Nathaniel Hawthorne was their neighbor. Louisa May's father, Bronson, was considered by both Thoreau and Emerson to have the greatest mind of the age. It was not, however, a very practical mind and it was to support her father that Louisa May wrote the girls' books which made her famous.

Below: A particularly popular site along Boston's Freedom Trail is the home of Paul Revere, built in 1677, almost 100 years before Revere occupied it. Revere was a talented silversmith who took part in the Boston Tea Party and helped spread propaganda against the British after the Boston Massacre. He was most famous for his role as chief rider, or message-bearer, for the local Committee of Safety before and during the Revolution.

The Philadelphia Library and the University of Pennsylvania owe their origins, albeit a little circuitously, to Franklin as well. Christ Church, located near Independence Hall, was built by money Franklin helped raise. Franklin is buried in the church's cemetery.

Just outside Philadelphia there is another important Revolutionary War site, Valley Forge. It is now an open park with an arch celebrating its past glory. The site's eye-appeal depends on the season, the more color the better. Winter is its least attractive time, an ironic truth since the fame of the place is based on George Washington's decision to establish his army's headquarters there during the winter of 1777–8. The deliberate determination that characterized the soldiers at Valley Forge was quite different from the spontaneous enthusiasm that exploded at Concord. Perhaps great tides of history need both emotion to set the spark and an ordered commitment to keep it going. Such commitment cannot be preserved in the scenery, but visitors to Valley Forge are usually stirred none the less. Recent archaeological work has discovered much about the site and new displays are being constructed to explain the nature of that winter.

Even richer than the region's history is the diversity of its people. Much of the north-east was first settled by persecuted religious groups. It began with the arrival of the Puritans and other Protestant radicals, but over the centuries hardly a religion in Europe has not been persecuted somewhere and the

Below left: The Amish are good and energetic farmers, although they refuse to plow with tractors or to use any other powered farm machinery. All the equipment they use on their farms is drawn by horses.

Below right: The old Pennsylvania State House, or Independence Hall, is Philadelphia's most popular visitor site. The Declaration of Independence was signed in this fine building on 4 July 1776.

Right: Fields plowed along the contours fill the Pennsylvania countryside with abstract patterns. Isolated groves of trees recall the time when the entire area was a rolling land of forests.

north-east now has many Catholics and Jews as well as minority Protestants. After the Civil War and for the first two-thirds of this century, blacks fleeing poverty and discrimination in the south migrated to the north-east. At present the greatest migration to the area comes from the West Indies. Puerto Rico was first and now Jamaica, Haiti, and other islands are contributing a large population to the region. The result of this mix is the modern Yankee: a person who is aware of his own heritage and alert to the fact that other people are also proud of their own backgrounds.

Originally each group may have hoped to retain its old identity and community without change, but by sharing jobs, ambitions, and local politics a New World version of the old cultures emerged. No matter what their former attitude was, in America each group's survival has required the urging of tolerance for all. Societies which elsewhere are separated by many national boundaries rub shoulders in the American north-east. Even speech is affected. Yiddish words, some German sentence structure, a tendency to give all romance-language names a Spanish pronunciation, and black slang are regular features of north-eastern speech and do not imply a particular heritage.

The blending of cultures takes place more readily in the cities and also depends in part on the energy with which the immigrants and their descendants assert their identities. The group most resistant to change has probably been the Pennsylvania Dutch who settled in the Susquehanna Valley around Lancaster and also near the Pocono Mountains. For almost three centuries these communities have maintained the austere faith of their forebears. Like the New England Yankees, the Pennsylvania Dutch are famous for being shrewd bargainers, industrious, frugal, and opposed to prideful displays. They are descended from radical Protestant groups which appeared in Germany during the 15th and 16th centuries. (The name 'Dutch' is English for the German *Deutsche*.) During the 18th century they came to Pennsylvania in their thousands. In those days street signs in Philadelphia were in both English and German, and Benjamin Franklin even wondered if the German language might not overwhelm English in Pennsylvania. A form of low German is still spoken by many of the Pennsylvania Dutch.

Most of these Germans did become part of the American melting pot, but a few groups have adhered firmly to the old principles. Most notable are the Amish who have been kept together by their practice of shunning both outsiders and members of the community who break their rules. Even now, they almost wholly ignore the outside world. The special nature of the Amish becomes apparent when a person travels through their farmlands. Their dress code is strict and sober and they do not use electricity. Telephone poles do not line the highways; electric wires do not lead up to the farmhouses. Instead of traveling by automobile, they ride in horse-drawn buggies. Farm machinery is horse-drawn too.

Although the Pennsylvania Dutch are unusual for the extent to which they have managed to preserve their special identity, they are a typical example of the kind of immigrant which the northeast has been getting since 1620. Minority groups with a strong personal code have come time and again. The first such immigrants were the Pilgrims. Like the Pennsylvania Dutch, they too belonged to a persecuted minority of religious radicals who asked no more of the world than to be let alone. In their case they were Separatists born in the Nottinghamshire village of Scrooby. Since they were the first to settle north of Virginia, they are remembered with a special affection in American history and Plymouth, Massachusetts, where they first settled, is a popular tourist site. The point where they came ashore, Plymouth Rock, is preserved as a national shrine.

More recently arrived groups include the Chassidim, a mystical Jewish sect from central Europe. The men, with their dark clothing, long curls, and beards can be seen every day going about their business in Manhattan and Brooklyn. Less visible but strongly group-conscious peoples include Portuguese in New Bedford, Massachusetts and French-Canadians in Maine.

These peoples have been brought together in a special way. They are a strange breed of cosmopolites who talk at length about their particular heritages. Yet they are indeed part of the New World rather than the Old. A man who brags of his Italian ancestors may have a German name; a Jew can love an Armenian. This unity which nevertheless retains diversity is the greatest strength of the region.

The Great Lakes

A handbook published in 1852 for travelers between Buffalo and Montreal urged visitors to Niagara Falls to ride the small ferryboat that crossed just below the falls, advising, 'It is from the center of the river that the falls are viewed as a *whole,* and the eye at one glance is enabled to rest upon them in their undivided grandeur and sublimity.'

The book had it right. There are many special views of the falls, but the one not to be missed is from below. Put on a raincoat (provided by the boat company) and sail into the teeth of the spray. That is the way to taste it, to feel the abundance of the earth's power as incredible, endless tons of water fall around you.

Niagara Falls is the greatest natural wonder in eastern America. It is located directly on the US–Canada border and along with this political division the falls are naturally divided by a narrow wooded strip of hard rock called Goat Island. An elevator on Goat Island carries visitors down to the Cave of the Winds where it is possible to walk between the rocks and the tumbling sheet of water. The American Falls are 167 ft (51 m) high and 1,075 ft (330 m) wide. The Canadian or Horseshoe Falls are generally considered the more spectacular since they are almost twice as wide, 2,100 ft (646 m). Engineers have also

calculated the average flow in cubic feet per minute, but such numbers are as meaningless as they are irrelevant. Niagara Falls is a reminder of what technology sometimes urges us to forget: nature is power, extravagant and unimaginable.

The sources of Niagara's strength are the inland seas that lie behind it. America's Great Lakes are unlike any other water system on earth; they are huge and huge again, containing one-fifth of the world's total standing fresh water. The astronauts could see them from the moon. They provide a water route from the Atlantic to the center of the North American continent and made early exploration of the interior relatively easy. The first lake encountered by European explorers was Ontario, smallest of the five that were ultimately to be found. Beyond Ontario was Niagara Falls and its immediate source, Lake Erie.

Discovery of this immense inland waterway revived hopes that a northern route to China might be found, and the French tried further exploration. Instead of China, they discovered three more lakes, each of them even larger than Erie. Lakes Huron, Michigan, and Superior all pinwheel out from the tip of Michigan state's Upper Peninsula and provide easy access to thousands of miles of shoreline. Superior, the biggest of them

Above: Michigan borders on four of the five Great Lakes. The state also contains 11,000 smaller lakes which encourage fishing, swimming, and relaxing around a campfire. This scenic splendor has made tourism the state's second largest industry. The forests that line many of the lakeshores have long been a source of hardwood timber for construction and for the manufacture of furniture.

Previous pages: Maid of the Mist Pool at the foot of Niagara Falls is calm enough to permit boats and even ducks.

Above right: The Niagara Frontier is a recreation area that stretches along the New York side of the Niagara River. Its most remarkable attraction is Niagara Falls which, from the American side, can best be viewed from Prospect Point. A footbridge out to Goat Island permits dramatic close-ups of the falls.

Below right: The Wisconsin Dells is a narrow gorge cut by the Wisconsin River and, for the past century, has been a popular resort. Visitors can ride an amphibious vehicle right through the depths of the gorge.

all, is the world's largest body of fresh water. It wasn't China, but it was a place rich in fur and souls worthy of salvation. Before William Penn founded his city of Philadelphia, the French had well-established mission chapels and trading routes throughout the Great Lakes.

The lakes' present form is, in geological terms, quite young. They were carved out by the last of the great ice-age glaciers, the Wisconsin. Travelers in the region find plenty of signs of its glacial history. Boulder fields such as the one around Traverse City, Michigan are filled with rocks carried in by the glaciers. Ice-carved grooves in rocks on Kelleys Island, Lake Erie are so sharply defined and polished that they look man-made. The Wisconsin glacier began its retreat only 12,000 years ago. The ice melted; the lake beds filled; Niagara began to trickle, and finally to roar.

Originally the waters of the Great Lakes were so pure they were the natural equivalent of distilled water, and some of this pristine wilderness survives today in the northern lakes, particularly along the shores of Lake Superior. Canoeing and backpacking are the best ways to see much of this country. There are also some good auto trails. One of the loveliest and wildest roads in the country is the 150 mile (240 km) shore drive north from Duluth, Minnesota to the Canadian border. Duluth itself is a busy port, but once the road passes Two Harbors its isolation and beauty is striking. Wild plunges are intrinsic to the scenes here. Gooseberry Falls, at 240 ft (75m), are higher than Niagara, and the lonely Split Rock lighthouse sits on a cliff that drops 170 ft (50 m) to the lake below.

On the inland side of the road is Superior National Forest, containing over 5,000 lakes. Minnesota, Wisconsin, and upper Michigan are pock-marked with tens of thousands of small and some not so small lakes. There are still several lifetimes' worth of exploring to be done in this lake district. Canoe trails are the only way to reach many of the area's islands and shores. One of America's newest and least known national parks, Voyageurs, is in this region, up at Rainy Lake on the Canadian border.

On the shore drive, just before reaching Canada, is the town of Grand Portage, so called because it was here that trappers

Far left: For centuries commerce was conducted throughout the inland seas by canoe. John Jacob Astor's fur traders used them and so did the Ottawa Indians who transported goods to places as widely separated as Green Bay, Wisconsin and Quebec, Canada. Today canoeing is still a popular sport in the rivers and streams that feed the Great Lakes.

Above left: The Straits of Mackinac (pronounced Mac-in-aw) divide Michigan's two peninsulas and unite Lakes Michigan and Huron. The straits are now crossed by the world's longest and strongest suspension bridge. From anchorage to anchorage the bridge is 7,400 ft (2,256 m). The pilings have been made extra strong to resist the ice which forms in the straits each winter. It must also survive intense winds and in 1955, while the bridge was still under construction, it withstood a hurricane-force storm.

Left: Originally the Erie Canal had 82 locks; these old ones are found at Lock Berlin, New York. Despite competition from the railroad and the St Lawrence Seaway, many sections of the old canal are still in use. They now comprise part of the modern New York Barge Canal System.

and traders used to leave Lake Superior to follow the fur trail to the west. Part of the old Grand Portage Trail is kept clear and visitors can walk along it. Also in Grand Portage is a boat for travel to Isle Royale, America's most primitive national park. Because of the difficulty of access it is also the least visited. No cars are allowed on the island, but there are many foot trails. The largest moose herd in North America, with over 400 members, lives amid the pine and spruce forests of Isle Royale. Mink and beaver also enjoy the island.

This immense wilderness once brought thousands of fur trappers into the Great Lakes. The French names found throughout the region are a souvenir of those trapping days and a few of the old trading forts still survive. The most important is on Mackinac Island, now a popular summer resort. In 1810 John Jacob Astor made Mackinac the headquarters of his North American Fur Company activities and his fort, which was actually built by the British 30 years before, still stands. It has been restored and is in fine condition. During its heyday the fort dealt with 2,000 trappers and *voy-*

ageurs, suppliers who traveled to the trading sites. It was the basis for the best known fortune in American history.

Today Mackinac is a summer island with one of the world's great resort hotels, the Grand. Built in 1887, the Grand Hotel has been kept in excellent repair and its 880 ft (270 m) long porch is surely what its owners claim: the longest in the world. Automobiles are banned from the island, so bicycles and horse-drawn carriages are common sights.

The island's great view is from the top of Sugar Loaf Rock, 284 ft (87 m) above the lake surface. This perch shows off the island's strategic location. Nearby are the Straits of Mackinac which link Lakes Huron and Michigan. On either side of the straits are the upper and lower Michigan peninsulas which once were the homes of thousands or perhaps millions of fur-bearing animals.

Directly opposite Mackinac, on the Upper Peninsula, is the town of St Ignace, founded as a Jesuit mission in 1671 by Father Jacques Marquette, the explorer of the Mississippi River. The ruins of a French fort are nearby and Marquette's

grave is in St Ignace. Not far away is Saulte Sainte Marie, the channel between Lakes Superior and Huron. It is a major passage point for ships and its great locks handle more tonnage every year than the Panama, Suez, and Kiel canals combined.

Modern canal-building technology was largely responsible for the tremendous urban development of the Great Lakes that has taken place during the past century and a half. Although white settlements were pushing across the whole length of the Appalachians by the time of the Revolution, there was an understandable reluctance on the part of many people to go too far back into the remote reaches of the interior where contact with the coastal civilization was so hard to maintain. The picture changed dramatically in 1825 when the Erie Canal was opened. It provided a continuous water route from the Atlantic coast to Lake Erie and made unification of the two regions economically possible. At Lockport, New York the old canal and its locks can still be examined. As soon as the canal

opened cities began to grow along the lake shores and they in turn promoted more inland development. Most of the major cities along the lakes were only chartered during the 1830s, but by the Civil War, only 30 years later, they had grown to be major population centers, foreshadowing the great importance of the area today.

The greatest city to rise along the lakes was Chicago. It is still the major transportation center in the United States. Its port is the most important one on the Great Lakes. Its railroad terminal is the world's largest and its airport, O'Hare, is thought to be the world's busiest. Quite reasonably, therefore, Chicago is regarded as the hub of much of the nation. Its convenient central location has made it a popular site for national conventions and meetings. Since 1860, when the Republicans met in Chicago to nominate Abraham Lincoln, 24 nominating conventions for the Presidency have taken place in the city.

But Chicago has made one great error. It took as its nick-

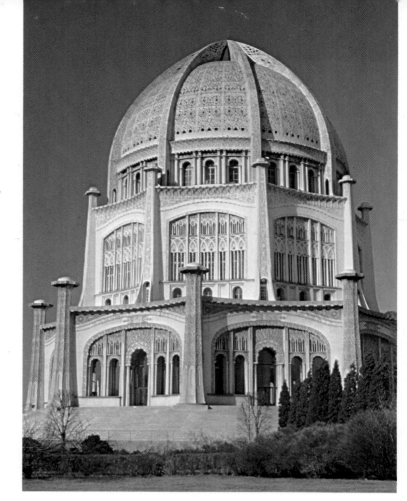

Right: The nine sides of the Baha'i Temple in Wilmette, Illinois, a suburb of Chicago, refer to mystical ideas which the Baha'i faith associates with that number. Baha'i is one of the world's newest religions; it was proclaimed in Persia during the mid-19th century by its prophet, Baha' Allah. Its principal doctrine is that God is unknowable because He cannot be described in human or material terms, but He speaks to the world through its great prophets. Included among these messengers of God are Abraham, Moses, Jesus, Mohammed, and Baha' Allah.

Left: It is not surprising that many different styles of skyscraper, ranging from highly decorated Gothic Revival to plain, simple, mainly glass buildings, are visible from Chicago's Sears Tower (the world's tallest building), since the fundamental uses and construction techniques of giant office buildings were all developed in Chicago during the late 19th century. At that time the Chicago School of Architecture was the most important in the country. Its most talented member, Louis Sullivan, is still considered the father of American architecture.

name 'The Second City,' a title that suggests Chicago is somehow not quite up to the mark. The impression is most unfortunate. Educationally, the University of Chicago has made as great a contribution to American thought as any school in the country. In letters Chicago has produced Theodore Dreiser, Carl Sandberg, and Nelson Algren. One of the very few living Americans to win the Nobel Prize for literature is Saul Bellow, a Chicago writer. Its Art Institute is splendid and its Museum of Science and Industry cannot be beaten.

It was Chicago that gave birth to America's most significant architectural innovation, the skyscraper. The first one was built there in 1883. Today the tallest building in the world is Chicago's Sears Tower. It stands 100 ft (30 m) taller than the twin towers of New York's World Trade Center. In fact, three of the world's five tallest buildings are in Chicago. From their heights the beaches and shipping of Lake Michigan are easily seen, reminding the observer of just what it was that made such wealth possible.

Above: The Ford assembly plant in Detroit, Michigan is the best known representative of the enormous manufacturing industry which lines the shores of the Great Lakes.

The Mississippi Basin

The Mississippi Basin

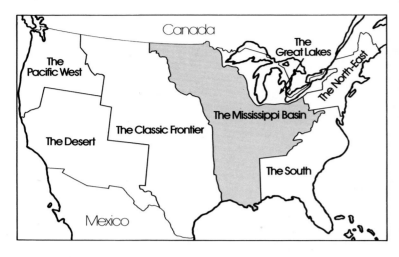

Great mounds built by the Indians are found throughout the valleys of the Mississippi, Missouri, and Ohio Rivers. The largest of them is Monk's Mound at Cahokia, Illinois, directly across the river from St Louis. This one mound covers 16 acres (6.5 hectares), is 100 ft (30 m) high and 1,080 ft (332 m) long. There are 85 mounds all told in Cahokia and at its peak the settlement there probably numbered about 10,000 people, making it one of the largest prehistoric cities in North America.

It is no accident that today there is a major city across from this ancient site. (Twenty-six mounds were leveled during the construction of downtown St Louis.) The location is one of tremendous natural value. The soils are fertile; the Mississippi River is immediately at hand; the land is high enough to avoid annual flooding and the site is between the confluences of the Mississippi's two major tributaries, the Ohio and the Missouri. The place is a natural crossroads of the continent.

Because of this strategic importance, many groups have sought to control or at least to have access to the Mississippi, and today the entire basin is filled with the symbols and traditions of many cultures.

French influence is pervasive at the river's delta. French-speaking 'Cajuns' still live in the swamps, or 'bayous' as they are called; radio stations broadcast in French and small-town cafés use French slogans to advertise national-brand beverages. The Cajuns are descended from the 'Acadians', French Canadians driven out of Nova Scotia by the British in 1755, who eventually settled in the swamp country near New Orleans. The nature of the land made farming difficult, so they lived mostly by hunting and fishing, and even today life in the bayous goes on in much the same way – lonely, isolated and remote. Much of the swamp region is still undeveloped and can be explored only by boat, although 'The Old Spanish Trail' does offer a memorable drive through the bayou.

Previous pages: Charles Dickens complained that the sternwheelers of America did not even look like boats, but they have now become symbols of America's old river traffic.

Far left: In the bayous of the Mississippi Delta (above) there are still Cajuns (below) who hunt and trap swamp animals for a living.

Above: Avery Island, on the Louisiana coast, has alligators, oil, groves of hot peppers, and great trees draped with Spanish moss.

The Mississippi Basin

The great city of the lower river, New Orleans, was built by a French explorer, the Sieure d'Bienville, on the first patch of dry land he could identify. New Orleans's most exciting and interesting section is still the old French Quarter. Its wrought-iron balconies and narrow streets provide an atmosphere of gracious good taste unlike any other American city. The classic way to visit the quarter is to, first, wander aimlessly along old streets with French names like Chartres and Royale. Then go over to Bourbon Street to enjoy some New Orleans jazz. Some time after midnight drop by the French Market and have some of the local coffee mixed with chicory. If all of this can be done during the week that preceeds Ash Wednesday, it will be a great experience indeed. Over a million visitors pack themselves into New Orleans for the festivities that climax on Mardi Gras and the city goes wild as people roam the streets in search of a good time.

New Orleans cooking is its own. The recipes have marvelous names like gumbo and jambalaya. A gumbo is a soup thickened with okra, while jambalaya is chicken with rice and Creole spices. At the northern end of town, next to Lake Pontchartrain, the main dish is crab, eaten with the fingers.

During the days of the Old South New Orleans was a major slave and cotton trading center. Following the Civil War the city was less active (although it was during that period that jazz was born), its economy began to revive after World War I and now it is bustling again. Its key has always been the Mississippi River. The port of New Orleans is the second largest in the nation and the third largest in the world.

The river at New Orleans and for almost 1,000 miles (1,600 km) to the north is the Mississippi of 'Ol' Man River' fame. It is wide, muddy, and constantly bending. Both sides are guarded by levees, large mounds built to control the river's floods. There are typical southern rural scenes along this stretch of the river, for these were all slave-holding states and fine old plantation houses are found on both banks; however, the presence of the river gave the area a special interest in commerce that was not shared by the rest of the southern system. The east bank of the river has a number of high bluffs where towns and cities could grow without fear of floods. Baton Rouge, Natchez, Vicksburg, and Memphis are all built on these bluffs at the river's edge.

At Cairo, Illinois the Ohio River flows into the Mississippi. The Ohio carries double the volume of the upper Mississippi and some quarrelsome geographers have suggested that actually the Mississippi flows into the Ohio. Culturally speaking, however, it seems clear that the Ohio joins the Mississippi, providing yet another influence in that central valley. While everybody—French, Spanish, British, and Americans—had a hand in shaping the society of the Mississippi, the modern Ohio was pretty near exclusively an American development.

Name something American! It will turn out to be intimately associated with the Ohio Valley. 'Apple pie,' you say? Sure, Johnny Appleseed wandered near the banks of the Ohio planting apple trees. Did I hear 'baseball?' It was at Cincinnati, second largest city on the river, that professional baseball first appeared. The Cincinnati Red Stockings, now called the Reds, are still there, playing at the modern Riverfront Stadium. A few miles downriver, at the Falls of the Ohio, is Louisville, home of the most famous horse race in the United States, the Kentucky Derby.

By now some musically inclined reader is fairly near to shouting that 'country and western' music is very American. Originally this music was called 'hillbilly style' and the hills

where those Billies played were along the southern banks of the Ohio and its tributaries. The music's commercial center is only about 100 miles (160 km) from the Ohio at Nashville, Tennessee. Nashville's chief tourist attraction is 'Opryland,' a theme amusement park where country music is king.

Still trying to think of something American to stump me? Sorry, George Washington won't do either. He was the first to scout the river's headwaters for the British army and became a lifelong enthusiast of western expansion and development along the Ohio. America's other hero-president, Abraham Lincoln, was born, raised, and lived most of his life in the valley; his memory is even now the greatest draw for most visitors to the region.

Above left: Carnival time in New Orleans witnesses endless days of celebration and parades. For natives of the city the festivities can begin as early as Twelfth Night. Parades and parties are organized by groups called 'krewes,' each of which selects a king to reign during its parade. The most prestigious group is the Rex Krewe whose parade climaxes Mardi Gras day.

Above: More ironwork survives in the buildings of New Orleans than anywhere else in the country. The old French Quarter is the only place where delicate lace patterns of iron often rise two and three storeys high.

Left: Gospel singing has been the most important influence in American music. The lyrics of popular songs can stray far from the spirit of their sources, but the sound of the blues, jazz, rock and roll, and country music all owe much to gospel songs, especially those in the tradition of black gospel singing.

Below: Abraham Lincoln's early home at Knob Creek, Kentucky is now a symbol of the humble origins of America's greatest leaders.

Right: The D'Evereux Mansion is one of the many

pre-Civil War Homes to see in Natchez, Mississippi.

Bottom: the New River links farmers like these tobacco-growers in West Virginia's Appalachians with the Ohio River valley.

Lincoln was born in Kentucky at the preserved Sinking Spring Farm, but his family soon moved and his earliest memories were of Knob Creek where there is now a reconstructed log cabin like the one he lived in. As a boy, aged 7 to 21, Lincoln grew up in Indiana close to the banks of the Ohio. The Lincoln Boyhood National Memorial and the Lincoln Pioneer Village commemorate those Indiana days. And as for Illinois, there hardly seems to be a place in the southern half of the state that was denied some role in his life. In Metamore the courthouse where the great man argued cases still stands. A restored frontier village at Lincoln's New Salem State Park shows the kind of pioneer land young Abe grew up in and the Lincoln Homestead State Park near Decatur marks the place where his family lived. Springfield, where Lincoln finally settled down in 1837 at the age of 28, has his home, his law office, and his grave.

The Civil War during which Lincoln was President brought a special agony to the Ohio Valley. More than anywhere else it was Lincoln's own territory that saw families and friendships

torn apart by the Civil War. Lincoln himself lost a good friend to the other side. Benjamin Hardin Helm, whose birthplace can be visited in Elizabethtown, Kentucky, married into the family of Lincoln's wife and became friendly with Lincoln. When the war broke out, Helm was offered the post of army paymaster, but he followed a different star from Lincoln's, joined the Confederate Army and was eventually killed at the Battle of Chickamauga.

To people who lived outside the valley, the Ohio River was viewed as an extension of the Mason-Dixon line, the great divide between slave and free states. Its symbol as a demarcation point was crystalized by Harriet Beecher Stowe in *Uncle Tom's Cabin* when the runaway slave, Eliza, was described fleeing across the ice in the Ohio to get to the river's northern bank. But the north side was not Yankee and the southern bank was not typical of the Old South. Cincinnati, north of the river, was generally sympathetic to slavery and Louisville, on the south shore, contributed a prominent citizen, James Speed, to Lincoln's cabinet. (Speed's home, Farm-

ington, was designed by Thomas Jefferson and can still be visited.) When the crisis came no state on the south bank of the Ohio seceded from the Union. Kentucky stayed loyal and West Virginia seceded from Virginia rather than break with the Federation.

Most of the Civil War was fought in the Mississippi basin and most of the battlefields are preserved as military parks. Shiloh and Chattanooga battlefields in Tennessee mark the key sites where the Confederate forces were pushed out of the Ohio Valley. Along the Mississippi the most important and probably the most interesting site is at Vicksburg, whose fall brought the whole of the Mississippi Valley into Federal control. The city was besieged for over a month and a half and the military park still surrounds the city. It fell on 4 July 1863, and Vicksburg did not celebrate the Fourth of July again until 1945, when patriotism and victory in Europe at last overcame old hatreds. Vicksburg itself is an attractive old city whose militarily valuable bluffs provide pleasant views down to the Mississippi below.

The Mississippi Basin

The pivot of all these struggles and cultures in the Mississippi basin was St Louis, currently the largest metropolitan area in the entire region. The French influence is visible in both the city's name (Saint Louis was a French king) and in the presence of a great cathedral. It is unusual for American cities to claim a cathedral as a tourist attraction, but the Basilica of St Louis, completed in 1834, is special. Particularly appealing are the many beautiful mosaics beneath its dome. The old river culture is also represented in the city, largely by the various steamboats down along the harbor. Some boats are floating restaurants, others give tours of the river. The modern culture that finally triumphed here is also well represented. St Louis has a good art museum, a particularly attractive planetarium, and a world-famous zoo that includes performing animal acts.

Another important and popular visitors' site in St Louis is the Old Courthouse. The building is an especially strong reminder of the crossroads position that St Louis occupies in American geography and history. West of the Ohio River there was no longer a clear natural border between America's north and south; thus, the admission of new western states was accompanied by increasingly fierce struggles over whether the new territories would be slave or free. As early as 1820 the problem was recognized as affecting St Louis and the rest of the state of Missouri. A compromise was worked out, but a generation later (1850) it needed patching up. Then in 1857 the Dred Scott decision was handed down in St Louis's Old Courthouse. This decision voided all the old compromises and made war inescapable.

Right in front of the Old Courthouse is St Louis's most famous attraction, the 630 ft (193 m) tall Gateway Arch. The arch was only constructed during the 1960s, but already it has made St Louis a major tourist center. The arch symbolizes the fact that it was St Louis which opened up the American west. When it was being constructed some people suggested that Kansas City or St Joseph might be more appropriate sites, but it was St Louis, taking advantage of its river connections, that explored and identified the best routes to the west. A sketch of one St Louis family hints at the story.

St Louis was founded in 1764 by a French fur trapper named Pierre Laclede, who arrived with his common-law wife, Marie Chouteau. Laclede's descendants kept the name Chouteau and it was the Chouteau family that first developed much of the western Mississippi basin. Their memory is preserved by names spread throughout the west. Oklahoma has a town near Tulsa named Chouteau. Montana has a Chouteau County and a town called Choteau. Pierre, South Dakota, the state capital, was named for Laclede's oldest son, Pierre Chouteau.

St Louis's access to the west has always been based on its proximity to the 'Mighty Mo,' the Missouri River. The line between 'back east' and the old west of frontier romances runs through the middle of that great current. Between Kansas City, Missouri and Riverdale, North Dakota, the river's east bank is farmland, an extension of the Illinois and Indiana prairie; the west bank is ranchland. The most spectacular and least developed parts of the river are higher up, in Montana, at the Breaks of the Missouri. There the river cuts through badlands which can hardly be crossed any way except by boat. White chalk cliffs drop down to the river. Still further upstream, near Helena, Montana, the river enters the Rockies at the 'Gates of the Mountains,' a 2,000-ft (600-m) gorge, and not far beyond are the headwaters of the Missouri. The river is formed by the union at this point of three rivers, the Jefferson, the Madison, and the Gallatin.

These days, naturally, much of the river has been dammed up in order to control flooding and promote navigation. The two largest earthen dams in the world sit across the Missouri. The largest is Oahe at Pierre, South Dakota; second largest is at Fort Peck, Montana. The lake behind the Fort Peck Dam is 180 miles (290 km) long, but it winds so much that it has 1,600 miles (2,500 km) of shoreline. The lake splits into two forks, backing up both the Missouri and the now misnamed Little Dry Creek. The shoreline along the lake has a number of camping sites and the area is still fairly well stocked with animal and bird life. It was the fur-bearing wealth of the river valley which first brought trappers and traders up the Missouri from St Louis. Another giant dam on the river is Garrison Dam in North Dakota. The huge lake behind it was named for Sakakawea, the Indian woman who guided Lewis and Clark fron the North Dakota region to the Pacific coast during their exploration of the Louisiana Territory and beyond.

The two largest cities on the river are Kansas City and Omaha, both of them important meat-packing centers for shipping beef raised west of the Missouri to the great markets east of the river. Kansas City was long joked about as the stereotype of a backwater likely only to impress yokels from even further west, but such sneering was based more on eastern ignorance than on anything substantial. Opinion has now changed. François Mauriac once astounded his readers by proclaiming Kansas City 'the most beautiful city in the world.' Even visitors whose enthusiasm for the place is a little more tempered will admit that Kansas City has more beauty than expected. Its baseball stadium has an astonishing set of foun-

Below: American football
evolved from rugby. Its chief
differences are an emphasis
on maintaining possession
of the ball and the use of
complex and precisely
worked out maneuvers to
advance the ball toward a
goal.

Left: During the pause
between halves of the game,
marching bands entertain
on the field. Performances
such as this one shown at a
Kansas City Chiefs game in
Arrowhead Stadium
emphasize spectacle and
coordination more than
music.

tains. Still more fountains combine with parks and Spanish-style buildings to create what is probably the most attractive shopping center in the nation, the Country Club Plaza. Kansas City's residential neighborhoods are also quite lovely.

There are also a number of towns along the river which once served as major jumping-off points for trails leading further west. The main such town on the lower Missouri was St Joseph. The Oregon Trail left from there and so did the Pony Express riders. The site where the riders began their journey is now marked by the Pony Express Stables Museum. It was also in St Joseph that the west's most famous outlaw, Jesse James, was killed. Living under the name of Mr Howard, he was shot in the back in 1882. The house where this happened is still standing today.

On the upper Missouri steamboats eventually traveled beyond the breaks as far as Fort Benton, Montana. Travelers arriving at Fort Benton proceeded either south to Montana's gold-fields or west to the Pacific. The old steamboat levee is preserved as a national landmark and the waterfront's appearance is not a whole lot different from its boom days. Many of the century-old buildings still stand.

The really imaginative explorer of the Missouri River, however, will go east instead of west and take a look at the upper Mississippi basin. Like the Ohio Valley, the upper basin is thought of as heartland America. It includes Hannibal, Missouri, birthplace of Mark Twain. In his two most popular stories, *Tom Sawyer* and *Huckleberry Finn*, Twain turned Hannibal into everyone's vision of small-town America.

The symbol of the whole region is sweet corn, the most

Above: Much of the pleasure
of the game is in its
pageantry. During play
cheerleaders jump, wave
'pom-poms,' and shout
encouragement to their
team.

59

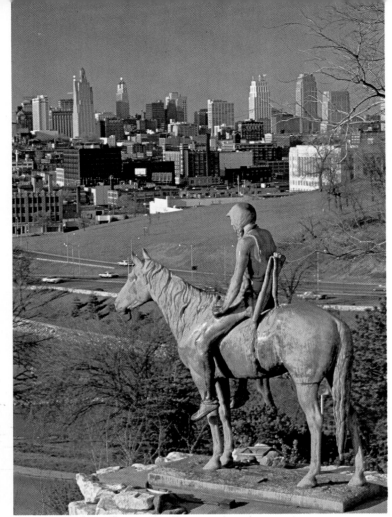

Far left: St Louis, with its arch symbolizing the opening up of the West, serves as a link between the Ohio and Missouri rivers.

Left: At Kansas City the Missouri River turns north while major roads and rail lines continue west.

Below left: The site of Minneapolis has changed greatly since the time described in Longfellow's poem 'The Song of Hiawatha.'
He wrote of a place
*   'Where the Falls of Minnehaha*
Flash and gleam among the oak-trees,
Laugh and leap into the valley.'

Below: Pittsburgh's business district, a group of striking buildings known as the 'Golden Triangle,' overlooks the point where the Allegheny and Monongahela rivers unite to form the Ohio.

American of vegetables. Mitchell, South Dakota even has a Corn Palace. This large building has mosaic murals made from corn kernels. Perhaps these decorations show the influence of St Louis on the upper basin, since the St Louis cathedral has such a splendid group of mosaics! Of course, the building is a tribute to the fertility of the earth. The country between the Missouri and the upper Mississippi rivers contains some of the world's richest farmland. Iowa's soil is so fertile that few farmers have been willing to abandon or sell it. In Iowa more property is still in the families of the original settlers than in any other state.

The upper basin is also a good place for observing wildlife, notably birds. The area is a great flyway for the many birds coming from or bound for Canada. The ancient migrations are a marvel to see; the sight of flock after flock coming down to land makes even the staunchest city-dweller glad to have found a hint of fresh air. East of Bismarck, North Dakota is an especially good area to watch the birds, although there are many other sites as well.

The great urban center of the upper basin is at the twin cities of St Paul and Minneapolis, Minnesota. They stand side by side, sharing the banks of the Mississippi, and they bustle with the tradition of growing heartland areas where commerce, civic pride, and art institutions are bound into one. Minneapolis's Tyrone Guthrie Theater is the best-known American stage company outside of New York. The cities boast of over a hundred parks with several dozen lakes for summer picnics, and during the winter there is a great Winter Carnival where a palace is sculpted in ice. Today the metropolitan area has a population of over two million people and is the headquarters for giant corporations both in traditional sectors of the economy like milling and mining and in space-age electronics as well.

The Twin Cities grew up next to the Falls of St Anthony (known to the Indians as the Minnehaha Falls), at the end of the navigable portion of the river. North of the falls the Mississippi narrows, although it is still 500 miles (800 km) from its source. Explorers interested in origins must travel through pine forests, a chain of lakes, and swamps before the ultimate source of the great river is found at Lake Itasca. As it leaves Itasca the Mississippi is only a few inches deep and is narrow enough to be crossed by a high school broad-jumper. It seems like one more tiny stream flowing from one of Minnesota's thousands of small lakes, but it is unique. It has a 2,315 mile (3,725 km) journey ahead of it. This little trickle of water holds the key to the center of the North American continent.

The Classic Frontier

The Classic Frontier

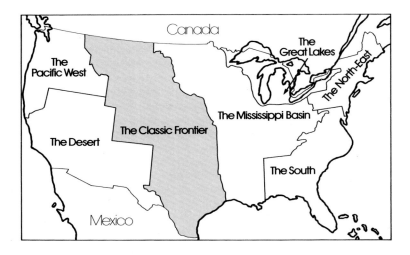

Previous pages: The harsh land sometimes triumphs. Calico, Colorado, was a silver mining center in the 1880s, but it is now a ghost town. Even the lake behind it has disappeared.

Right: The prairie extends all the way from the Missouri River to the Rocky Mountains.

Below: Windmills irrigate the dry Texas prairie.

Wide open spaces are what travelers find if they go west from the Missouri River to the Continental Divide or south from Kansas City toward the Pecos River. Americans have a lot of names for this region. Call it the plains, the range, or the prairie. In Russia it would be called a steppe; in southern Africa, a veld. This giant savanna grassland is not a desert, although it was long called The Great American Desert, but neither is it much in the way of good farmland. The real desert is still to the west, while the American breadbasket is back east. There are certainly farms, even some very large ones, but the plains are better suited as ranchland. Once, with nobody even trying, they supported millions of free-roaming buffalo. Today the plains hold cattle, millions of head. In fact the region has about twice as many beeves as people.

Something else is out there – oil. Texas, Oklahoma, Kansas, North Dakota, Wyoming, and Colorado are all important oil

suppliers. The oil economy of the plains states is probably best symbolized by Oklahoma City. Forty years after it was established the city was found to be directly on top of an enormous gas and oil field. Today pumps and derricks are as much a part of the city as buildings and roads.

This region was long ignored by American pioneers looking for new land to settle. After the upper Mississippi basin was occupied Americans skipped over these central plains and headed for Oregon. In those days the plains were considered a kind of inland sea. Flat, relatively easy to cross, endless, and monotonously unchanging, the plains were navigated according to the stars and the wagons built for the journey were called 'prairie schooners.' Today, too, there is a tendency for travelers crossing the region to try to establish speed records for the passage, but the highways nevertheless do offer some surprising scenery.

A typical example is the route of US Highway 14 through southern South Dakota and northern Wyoming. The highway leaves the Missouri River at Fort Pierre and soon enough begins to cross the Badlands. A long time ago this region, too, was flat grassland, but then the wonders of geologic pressures went to work. The land began to rise and most of it was slowly washed or blown away, leaving a sterile and empty country full of rock columns too hard to be fully eroded. There is no vegetation in the Badlands, but a few coyotes live there along with some jack rabbits and prairie dogs. The area used to be rich in wildlife, and fossils of sabre-toothed tigers, camels, rhinoceroses, and three-toed horses have been found embedded in the rocks.

An hour's drive west of the Badlands National Monument are Rapid City and the Black Hills. These hills are low mountains of solid granite; the stone is tough enough to have

The Classic Frontier

resisted the forces which eroded the Badlands. Although the hills have many scenic foot and horse trails, the one sight every passer-by wants to see is the man-made Mount Rushmore National Memorial. Giant heads, each 60 ft (18.5 m) high, have been sculpted out of the mountain face. Dynamite more than a sculptor's chisel was needed for a project this huge carved in stone this hard. The work was a triumph of explosives technique and the result was a fully recognizable set of heads representing Presidents Washington, Jefferson, Lincoln, and Theodore Roosevelt.

Near Mount Rushmore is Deadwood Gulch and the Old West town of Deadwood. For a place with only one street it draws an awful lot of visitors. It was in Deadwood that Wild Bill Hickock was murdered while playing poker. He and another Old West celebrity, Calamity Jane, are buried in the town graveyard.

The chief river in this area is the Belle Fourche, or 'Beautiful Fork' of the Cheyenne River. The French name is a reminder that this area, too, was first explored by fur traders coming up from St Louis. The town of Belle Fourche is at the northern entrance to the Black Hills; nearby is the geographic center of the United States.

The Belle Fourche River and US Highway 14 both pass close by the Devil's Tower National Monument, an astonishing butte that rises from a pine forest to stand by itself 865 ft (266 m) above the plain. The tower is all that remains of an extinct volcano. Once again the enormous erosive powers in this region have carried off all the soft parts of the mountain, leaving only the central rock core. Anyone who is mountaineer enough to reach the tower summit will find chipmunks and small birds there to greet him. The view is something special. The Black Hills are to the southeast while the Wyoming flatland stretches south and west, apparently to the edge of the world.

The highway begins to cross an enormous alkaline flat. The words of an old cowpoke song might have been written for this place:

Oh, give me a home
  Where the buffalo roam
And the deer and the antelope play,
Where seldom is heard
  A discouraging word
And the skies are not cloudy all day.

But of course the buffalo are gone now, remembered only in a few place names. One town is called Buffalo and another is named Cody, after William Cody or, as he was more popularly known, 'Buffalo Bill.' As for deer and antelope, well, the highway does cross the Bighorn Mountains, named for bighorn sheep, and some wildlife can be encountered there. The wildest area is in the great gorge of the Bighorn River as it cuts through the range. These mountains are not just hills; they are a thin, tall ridge hinting that something is happening. The plains are slowly being crossed; half of Wyoming is now behind the traveler, and up ahead, just before reaching the state border, lies the Continental Divide. The divide is the major watershed line in North America, separating water which will eventually reach the Pacific from water bound for the Gulf of Mexico and the Atlantic.

As a general rule the divide runs through the Rocky Mountains and this area holds true to form. Beyond the town of Cody the Rockies stand tall; the highway enters them and Yellowstone National Park at Sylvan Pass. The mountains are attractive, but it is water that holds the key to the wonders of the Yellowstone. Isa Lake, in the park, is usually covered with

water lilies and does not look like much, but it straddles the Continental Divide and its waters eventually reach both the great river of the east, the Mississippi, and of the west, the Columbia.

The most famous wonders in Yellowstone are its numerous geysers – eruptions of steaming water. A geyser is akin to a pressure cooker. Beneath the Yellowstone terrain are great seas of water stored under pressure and at temperatures much hotter than the normal boiling point. Eventually the pressure grows too strong and the water erupts through the earth like steam escaping through a valve. Yellowstone has 300 geysers, more than 50 per cent of the world's total. The most famous of the park geysers is Old Faithful. It erupts, on the average, every 65 minutes and climbs to a height of about 130 ft (40 m). The eruption lasts for several minutes and most of the water drains into the Firehole River. Since the Firehole leads to the Madison River which helps form the Missouri River which joins the Mississippi, and since Old Faithful is only a few miles from the Continental Divide, this world-famous geyser is a source for one of the longest water journeys on earth.

Just below Yellowstone is Grand Teton National Park. Looking like Switzerland, the Tetons are a ridge of mountains which stand over a small savanna called Jackson's Hole. It is a place of great beauty, long remembered by astonished travelers bound for the more famous Yellowstone area. Fur traders and Indians used to rendezvous in Jackson's Hole to trade and talk. One look at the grassy plain ringed by purplish mountains tells the visitor that those old traders really did know the secret routes to Eden.

Besides Yellowstone, two other national Parks are set squarely on the Continental Divide: Glacier National Park, Montana and Rocky Mountain National Park, Colorado. Glacier is the more formidable of the two, being almost four

Left: About 70 million gallons (over 260 million litres) of hot water gush forth in Yellowstone each day. Most of it emerges in a steady stream at places like the dramatic terraces of Minerva Springs.

Below: Considered by some to be the most remarkable monument built since the ancient Egyptians, the Mount Rushmore memorial, carved from the granite rock, was constructed between 1927–42.

Above: South Dakota's Badlands are an enormous area of eroded gullies and buttes. Indians and trappers called the region 'the bad lands to cross.'

Right: Old Faithful's regularity and height has made it America's best known geyser. Geyser eruptions are rare outside Yellowstone National Park.

times larger. Most of the park must be explored either on foot or on horseback. One popular all-day hike is from the Many Glaciers Hotel up to Grinnell Glacier and back. The glacier has made a long retreat during the past quarter-century and hikers can see the high polish of the newly exposed glacier beds. Rocky Mountain Park is best known for its Trail Ridge Road, an auto highway among the mountain peaks. Fifteen miles (24 km) of the road are above the timberline.

The Colorado Rockies have established themselves as great ski resorts. Aspen, Vail, and Crested Butte are world famous, but there are plenty of other ski slopes as well. One popular resort is Loveland Pass, due west of Denver and right on the Continental Divide. Many skiers love the setting and atmosphere of the resorts as much as the sport itself. The warm chalets at the foot of snow-covered slopes are full of life and good company. The scenes of rugged peaks with their plays of light and color also win admirers who would never try to ski.

Although these ski areas are in the mountains, they are also at the edge of the plains. The Colorado Rockies simply burst forth from the savanna. Colorado's capital city of Denver is less than 60 miles (95 km) from the Continental Divide and yet it sits on a smooth plain. On smogless days the mountains can be seen in the distance, but they are only a backdrop. Denver's initial wealth was based on gold found in the South Platte River, but the city grew to be more than just another mining town because it served as a hinge between the mountains and the plains. It was a transport point for gold and other minerals coming out of the mountains just to the west and a receiving station for eastern goods needed by mountain prospectors. Denver has taken advantage of its natural attractiveness by developing the largest system of public parks and recreational facilities of any city in the world. The most appealing of the parks is the Denver Botanic Garden.

The other great metropolis of the plains is in Texas, at Dallas-Fort Worth. These two cities were once a day's ride apart, but they have been growing towards one another. The

Far left: It was mineral wealth that first drew large numbers of white men to the Rocky Mountains. Gold and silver were the earliest riches to excite prospectors, but the Rockies are so thick with metals that much else is mined there. Copper is its most valuable metal today and most of America's uranium and molybdenum lies in the Rockies. When some other metal turns out to be important, the chances are strong that it too will be found in the Rockies. Ouray, Colorado, at the western end of the San Juan Range of the Rockies is a typical old gold-mining town that has become a resort. The San Juans are the source of the Rio Grande. Their majestic peaks are among the tallest in the Rockies; many reach over 14,000 ft (4,300 m).

Left: The highest of all the Rockies is Mt Elbert – 14,431 ft (4,399 m) – which stands near America's most famous ski resort, Aspen, Colorado. During the 1880s Aspen was one of the world's greatest silver mining towns and the local excitement was looking for pay-dirt (prospecting). Today it comes from downhill races like the head-to-head slalom in which two skiers race along parallel courses.

merging has been encouraged by the sharing of many facilities, notably the enormous airport and many tourist and recreation projects. Promoters eager to tap both the Fort Worth and Dallas markets have built in the town of Arlington, whose claim to prominence was that it lay midway between the two big cities. Arlington now boasts a huge theme amusement park, a major-league baseball team, a marine park, a safari park, golf courses, and hotels of every class. The Dallas football stadium is also nearby. The catalyst behind the development of Arlington was the 'Six Flags Over Texas' theme park which opened in 1961. The park stresses visitor participation: six-gun shootouts are routine events along the sidewalks of the park and an armed bandit may even tell visitors to 'stick 'em up!'

Visitors from Mars might be astonished by such violent goings-on, but anyone from a slightly less remote locale already knows the true attraction of the plains states. They were the site of the classic western legend of America. At some point in its history every part of America was the frontier—that is, the edge of the settlement—but it was the frontier of the 1870s and '80s that managed to lodge itself in the American mind as 'The Frontier.' The western states of that classic period are Texas, Colorado, Wyoming, Montana, North Dakota, South Dakota, Nebraska, Kansas, and Oklahoma.

The reason the land was so slow to be occupied has already been noted. It is flat, not terribly fertile, and given to sudden expanses of worthless erosion. Half a century after it was settled it turned into the 'Dust Bowl.' Overgrazed and overplowed, it just seemed to dry up and blow away. Even today the region is not terribly populous. It comprises about a quarter of the United States territory and contains only 10 per cent of the people.

The story of the region's settlement, however, is now firmly lodged in American mythology and travelers who move away from the edges of the plains out towards the center are almost invariably looking for one or more parts of that tale. The plains

69

were the West of the cowboys, the Indian Territory, and the herds of wild buffalo. When we talk about places beyond the Continental Divide we speak of the 'north-west,' and beyond the Pecos River it is the 'far west.' The 'west' plain and simple is the old frontier area with Dodge City in the center, the site of Custer's Last Stand in the north, and the Texas longhorn cattle trails in the south.

Since the area is so huge, it is impossible to explore the whole country for its frontier lore, but there are two rules of thumb. If the Old West of the Indians most excites you, visit Oklahoma. If it is the Old West of the settlers you are interested in, head for Dodge City, Kansas. Whatever else can be squeezed in is so much extra pie.

During much of the 19th century Oklahoma was the Indian Territory, and it still has the largest Indian population in the country. Some 35 tribes are represented there. Their original lands were throughout the present United States. Cherokee from the Carolina Appalachians, Seminole from Florida, Delaware from New York, Pawnee from Nebraska, Modoc from California, and even Ottawa from Canada were among the tribes which were moved to the territory. The concentration of such numbers on savanna grassland made it impossible for the Indians to support themselves and they were completely dependent on aid from the federal government. The situation improved somewhat during this century, when it turned out that their apparently worthless land had quite a bit of oil under it.

One of the best places to see what the present-day Indians are like is southwest of Oklahoma City at Andarko. The town has many museums, craft shops, and year-round ceremonial dances. In August Andarko hosts the American Indian Exposition which draws many Indians and white tourists. The Indians at the exposition are concerned with blending the new and the traditional.

In traveling through the old frontier states there is one quiet experience which should not be missed. Sit with friends or family in an Indian tepee and have a conversation. Since tepees could be dismantled, transported, and reassembled with relative ease, they were perfect lodgings for nomadic peoples, but what is important for the modern visitor is the noble space they establish. People who sit in one are close enough to talk comfortably, but nobody has to be crowded. The walls create an effect similar to that of a Gothic cathedral; they enclose, but by soaring up beyond the line of sight they do not give a sense of confinement. A few minutes spent talking quietly in a tepee can provide a strong physical realization of the Indian sense of community.

The very opposite spirit, one of rugged individualism, is the cornerstone of the American western story. Lonesome cowboys, the solitary good guy confronting a pack of gunfighters, and the brave wagon alone on the prairie are images that haunt the American imagination and bring thousands of visitors each summer day to Dodge City in southern Kansas.

Dodge has two points of interest for visitors. There is a replica of Old Front Street and the Long Branch Saloon where cattle drovers, outlaws, and tough sheriffs all hung out. The old army outpost, Fort Dodge, has also been preserved and restored. The fort is interesting for both its sense of what those old forts were really like (not very elegant) and for the fact that Fort Dodge really was established so the cavalry could ride to the rescue of travelers surrounded by raiding Indians.

The old Santa Fe Trail crossed the Arkansas River near the site of Dodge City. The Santa Fe Trail was more of a caravan

Left: Cowboy outfits are not just costumes on a Texas ranch. The hat guards against the sun; blue jeans have to withstand mud and rough wear; while a coarse vest serves as a very necessary wind shield.

Below left: The most famous battle of Texas' war for independence from Mexico was the 12-day siege of the Alamo mission in San Antonio. On 6 March 1836 all 200 defenders were killed by Mexican troops.

route for traders than it was a trail for pioneers planning to settle in the west, and wagons along the trail tended to be loaded with valuable merchandise. They were tempting targets for the Indians and the point where the trail crossed the river was a particularly good location for attack. So Fort Dodge was established in order to strengthen this vulnerable spot on the route.

Travelers in Kansas, Wyoming, and South Dakota are sometimes astonished to encounter wagon trains still making their way across the plains. No, it is not a group of pioneers slow to learn of automobiles; there are companies which offer summer trips on a wagon train. Rides generally last from three days to a week and usually trace part of an actual western trail. Some companies even have Conestoga wagons of the sort used by the pioneers on their westward crossing.

The Oregon Trail was the most famous route through the plains. It crossed Nebraska and Wyoming before entering the Rockies at the South Pass and can be partly followed today by travelers on US Highways 30 and 26. Important trail sites that can still be visited include Fort Kearny, Scotts Bluff, Chimney Rock, and Fort Laramie. The South Pass is now a bit off the standard trail. Once it was the only route available for wagons trying to cross the Rockies, but now only a small state road leads there. The view is still impressive, however, and travelers have the impression that the far west has suddenly been spread out before them like a banquet at a table.

When the plains began to be settled rather than merely crossed, it was soon discovered that Fort Dodge had a second reason for being strategically valuable. It was plumb in the middle of the buffalo migration route—in fact, the first name for Dodge City was Buffalo City. The American buffalo, called the bison everywhere else in the world, once roamed the plains in their millions. The best estimates are that the territory of the present US once held 70 million buffalo. On the grasslands of the west the buffalo moved seasonally to fresh pastures, and the scenes of their movement never failed to astonish and impress. Travelers reported that 'the world looked like one robe,' but by 1889 only about 700 of the animals had survived the hunters.

Dodge City was a key location in the destruction of the buffalo population. Its position on the migration route made it a good place for hunters to assemble, and once the railroad line reached Dodge the town became a major shipping point. Millions of hides and thousands of tons of buffalo meat were sent east from Dodge.

Today the largest area still available to the buffalo is the Wichita Mountains Wildlife Refuge in southern Oklahoma. Like the Black Hills, the Wichita Mountains are granite peaks which jut up from the flatland and are too hard to have been blown away by the ceaseless wind. In 1907, 15 buffalo were brought there from a zoo in New York City; they did well, and now about 700 buffalo are established in the refuge along with about 300 longhorn cattle, plus elk, deer, prairie dogs, and wild turkey. Other important places to see buffalo are at Fort Niobrara National Wildlife Refuge, Nebraska, Custer State Park, South Dakota, and Montana's National Bison Range.

The destruction of the buffalo made the range lands available to cattle and Dodge City once again found it held a key location for the new enterprise of the plains. The railroad could carry cattle just as easily as it could buffalo hides. The great cowboy activity of legend was the driving of cattle from Texas up to a railhead. Those trails were hundreds of miles long and nothing close to such huge drives still exists; however, on large

Top: Well into the 19th century buffalo herds 4 million strong migrated across the plains. Their paths were circular, taking them north in the summer and bringing them 400 miles (640 km) south of those pastures for the winter. There are very few buffalo left today.

Above: The Cherokee was once the dominant tribe of the southern Appalachians, but white pressure for their land became irresistible during the 1830s when gold was found in their territory. The tribe was forced to emigrate to what is now Oklahoma, to land which no-one else then wanted.

Left: Scattered throughout
the west are old towns with
buildings which suggest the
place once bustled with
money. The brick and
ironwork of skilled artisans
survive and the high
ceilings recall a generous
spaciousness that has now
grown rare.

Below: Records prove that
cowboy-skill contests took
place out west before 1850.
During the 1870s they
became common parts of
Fourth of July celebrations
in cattle towns. Today
rodeos are festivities in their
own right and always begin
with a parade.

ranches cattle do still have to be moved from one pasture area to another and in some cases people who are willing to pay for the privilege are allowed to participate in a cattle drive. Normally the drives cover only short distances and take only a few days, but that is enough time to acquire a few saddle-sores and to say truthfully that you have done it. Colorado ranches in particular seem to welcome such guests. The greatest cattle drive a 'dude' (temporary cattle-hand) can participate in these days is the August drive of the Sweet Grass Ranch in Montana. The drive covers about 100 miles (160 km) and puts real demands on the riders.

Visitors who are eager to see cowboy skills being demonstrated, but who are not quite so interested in working up a heavy sweat, do best to attend some of the many rodeos held in the region. Rodeos are now organized athletic contests, but cowboy skills are still at the heart of the event, most notably the calf-roping contest and riding the bucking bronco. Calf-roping is a necessary part of ranch work since all calves must be caught, tied still, and branded.

In the Old West days, when it was more common to capture and ride wild horses, being able to ride a horse until it gave up fighting was a valuable skill. Bronco riding is a lot more dangerous than calf-roping and the symbol of the rodeo is undoubtedly that of the cowboy holding his hat high in the air while sitting on the arched back of an enraged horse.

There is no problem in finding a rodeo or two during a summer's drive through the old frontier states. They are everywhere. The peak season is July, but June and August see plenty of them too. Most towns of any size manage to hold a 'Frontier Days' festival big enough to fill at least a weekend. The rodeo which can be counted on to draw all of the top contenders for the championship title is the one held annually in Cheyenne, Wyoming during the third week in July. Dodge City Days are held around the same time.

The Dodge City boom as a cow-town lasted from 1872 to '82. During those ten years the legend that would last a century at least was established. Lawmen like Wyatt Earp and Bat Masterson used their guns pretty freely to keep bored cowboys and assorted desperados under control. It is a period which is relived among the replications of modern Dodge, but when the glory days passed Dodge did survive. Other towns were not so fortunate. They boomed and were then abandoned to become ghost towns. While such cities are scattered throughout the west, the most interesting ghost-town area is in Montana, south-east of Butte, where Bannack and Virginia City are to be found.

Bannack was the first territorial capital of Montana. Many of its buildings are in fairly good repair and still line the main street. The old territorial capitol stands along with a schoolhouse, a church, and some log cabins. The effect produced by the scene is the troubling one felt by travelers looking at the Roman Forum. The impermanence of the world, of even the most solidly constructed institutions, disturbs the soul and wakes the sleeper.

Montana's capital after Bannack was Virginia City, now billed as the 'Williamsburg of the West.' Thanks in large part to an interested millionaire, Virginia City has been restored to show the life of the place during the 1860s when the area was rich in gold mines and spendthrift prospectors. Virginia City is now so busy as a tourist center that it is no longer a ghost town, but its buildings and museums do offer a fine sense of what everyday life along the old frontier was like.

Left: The wild horses of the
old west were descendants
of horses brought to the
Americas by Spanish
conquistadors.

73

The Pacific West

The north-west surprises people with its cosmopolitan air and Yankee values. Oregon, Washington, Idaho, and northern California all boast of their western location, but the pioneers who first came to the region were not cowboys nor ranchers. Typically, they were relocated New Englanders, a fact reflected in place-names. The largest city in Oregon was named after Portland, Maine and the state capital after Salem, Massachusetts. Oregon even has old covered bridges. But the physical setting these newcomers found was completely unlike the northeast.

Great mountains rise one behind the other across the whole region. The coast itself is guarded by a line of steep mountains and rocky walls. A second, even greater ridge parallels the first. Behind these walls still more mountains bend and curve in capricious manner. They tangle and push inland to the Rockies and the Continental Divide. For those of us who are not mountain goats, it is a difficult land to cross.

It is also a beautiful land, with something new behind each fold in the earth. The tiny coastal sliver, for example, is a place of enormous trees. Most beautiful of these giants are the redwoods. The tallest tree in the country is believed to be in the Redwood National Park along the coast of northern California. It climbs to an altitude of 368 ft (113 m). Of course such size cannot be much appreciated by creatures whose heads poke only five or six feet above the ground. The stronger appeal of these forests is in their color, their rippled textures, and in the play of light. The massive trunks could almost be abstract paintings.

The forests support great logging industries, and coastal towns like Eureka, California, Coos Bay, Oregon, and Forks,

76

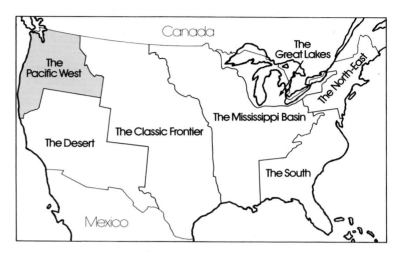

Left: The great sequoias of Redwood National Park, California are supported by the fog which comes in from the sea. The trees' brilliantly colored bark is 12 in (30 cm) thick and resists fire, fungus, and insects.

Far left: The harsh beach at Battle Rock State Park, Oregon is typical of America's Pacific coast.

Below left: Sea lions bask on the rocky coast of Oregon.

Washington are all based on timber. A visit to Forks gives a good idea of what such country is like. Forested slopes overlook a small, rough-and-tumble town. The two-lane highway is busy with superpowered trucks able to carry four or five giant trees to the lumber yards, and the hum of saws is coming from somewhere in the distance. Most people do not get terribly excited about vegetation, but when they get a look at the river of trees along the Pacific coast there is sometimes a tendency for the breath to catch. Can there really be so much tall wood in the world?

Part of the reason the forests are so thick is because of the rainfall—so much rain, in fact, that in a few places the forest has turned into jungle as dense as those along the Amazon and Congo Rivers. The Olympic National Park, next to Forks, contains several rain forests where the thick vegetation cannot be penetrated without a machete. Outside the park, south of Forks, along the Hoh River is another rain forest. The undergrowth is particularly heavy there as ferns, moss, and trees compete for every square inch of sunlight.

The forests are squeezed between a jagged coast and steep mountains. The northern end of the shoreline is included in the Olympic National Park, and since the beach is protected a few bald eagles still live among its cliffs and in the treetops. Large monoliths stand out in the ocean, marking where the coast once reached, and during low tides hikers can walk under a natural arch to learn what lies beyond.

The Pacific shores were once rich in seals and sea otters, whose fur drew ships from as far as Boston. Sea otter pelts brought the New England merchants a good price in China. A good place to find seals today is at Three Arch Rocks National Bird and Sea Lion Refuge on Cape Meares, Oregon. A sea lion is a seal with fairly small visible ears. Sea otters were once feared extinct, but have reappeared; they can often be seen in the water south of Port Orford, Oregon.

Another attractive coastal area is just north of San Francisco at the Point Reyes National Seashore. Francis Drake is believed to have sailed into the local bay during his round-the-world voyage. A good footpath leads down to the water, and the whole area is rich in wildflowers. When they are in bloom the colors are strong and varied enough to turn every photographer into an impressionist.

The reason for the wildness of the coast is in the mountains which leap up from the seashore. On the east side of the country the Coastal Range would be most impressive, a rival for the Appalachians, but in the west they seem rather diminutive. The most striking group is the Olympic section in the north. The peaks are not terribly high—Olympus, the tallest, reaches only 7,965 ft (2,428 m)—but they are treeless on top and have over 60 glaciers. Thus they give the effect of being much taller than they really are.

Previous pages: In 'Two Years Before the Mast' (1840) Richard Henry Dana prophesied, 'If California ever becomes a prosperous country, San Francisco Bay will be the center of its prosperity. The abundance of wood and water; the extreme fertility of its shores; and its facilities for navigation all fit it for a place of great importance.' He was right. The bay beyond the Golden Gate Bridge is today the commercial center of the Pacific.

Top: During the 1970s San Francisco's downtown area saw the sudden construction of giant office buildings which dramatically changed the city's appearance. The unique 48-storey pyramid shape of the Transamerica Building has become the symbol of this new look. The city's surrounding bay is one of the finest natural harbors in the world, so well protected that it seems to have first been discovered by inland explorers. The 8 mile (13 km) San Francisco-Oakland Bay Bridge system contains 2 double-deck suspension bridges, a tunnel through Yerba Buena Island, a cantilever bridge, and a viaduct leading into the city of Oakland.

Above left: The Sonoma and Napa valleys just north of San Francisco Bay contain America's finest vineyards. The California wine industry was almost ruined by the national prohibition of alcoholic sales (1919–33), but during the past 15 years it has recovered its sales and quality.

Above: San Francisco's Chinatown covers 12 square blocks, contains about 40,000 people, and is popular with tourists for its restaurants and many small shops. The quarter continues to receive new Chinese immigrants; today most come from Hong Kong.

Top right: The Seattle Center was the site of the 1962 Seattle World's Fair. The 74 acre (30 hectare) development is most famous for its Space Needle, Opera House, and fountains. Seattle itself serves as a major sea link with Alaska and the Far East. It is expected to be a key shipping point in the growing China trade. Since Seattle's protected harbor in Puget Sound is the equal of San Francisco's, the city began to boom as soon as a railroad line was able to reach it in 1892.

Below left: The campus of
Stanford University in
Paolo Alto, California is one
of the loveliest in America.
It was originally designed
by Frederick Olmstead, the
architect of New York City's
Central Park.

walls so sheer that they seem far from the urban world.

Because of the steepness of the hills, few people walk all over the city. They drive to Fisherman's Wharf for a look at all the wares on display and then drive over to the top of Telegraph Hill for a look at the bay and the Golden Gate Bridge. Often the main part of the bridge is wrapped in fog while the tops of its towers rise above the clouds to permit dramatic pictures. After a quick look it is back into the car for a drive to the Pacific Ocean side of town. Seals can be spied out on Seal Rock. In the evening there is a choice of opera, theater, symphony, or perhaps just a fine meal in one of the city's many restaurants. This combination of urban sophistication and spectacular views has made San Francisco the city in America everyone seems to love.

Most other important cities of the Pacific West are further inland, in the series of magnificent valleys which lie just beyond the coastal mountains. The prettiest is surely the Willamette Valley of Oregon. It is not large—much too small to contain any of the north-east's urban strips—but the soil is fertile, the surrounding mountains climb to snow-capped beauty, and many fine structures—notably covered bridges and Victorian mansions—grace the valley foreground. In the days of the pioneers the Willamette Valley was the goal of the thousands who crossed the Oregon Trail, and it still contains all of Oregon's major cities.

The special charm of the Willamette Valley is in its rural places. The Willamette River meanders freely and rewards the travelers who follow it upstream from Portland. The river is sluggish and dreamy along most of its length, though there are falls at Oregon City. Between Aurora and Champoeg the Willamette goes through French Prairie, the oldest white settlement area in Oregon and still a place of small farms. Like so much of the United States, this area was first explored by French-speaking trappers; more unusual is the fact that the valley was so luscious many of them abandoned trapping to start planting.

The valley disappears south of Eugene, but a similar one is found around the Sacramento River in northern California. During the 19th century the valley was a great wheat-basket, but overplanting and inattention to crop rotation destroyed the soil. Modern techniques, however, have put the valley back into production and great fields treat the traveler's eye. As with the Willamette Valley, the beauty along the Sacramento is enhanced by the high mountain walls which guard the distant horizon.

A third inland valley is the northern extension of the Willamette which reaches up to Puget Sound and Seattle. Seattle is the largest of the inland cities and this whole area is the most urbanized of the valleys. The best view of Seattle and Puget Sound is had from the top of the Space Needle. This 606-ft (186-m) tower was constructed for a World's Fair held in 1962 and its revolving restaurant at the top is still a great attraction. Seattle is built on the east side of Puget Sound, an inrush of the Pacific Ocean. The Olympic Mountains stand across the water and are splendidly visible on cloudless days. Directly behind Seattle are the Cascade Mountains, almost twice as tall as the Olympics. The city itself adds little in the way of beauty to the scene, but like San Francisco it is a place of sophistication and culture. Its best known and most important cultural event is the annual opera festival; Seattle is the only place outside of Germany where Wagner's complete Ring cycle is performed annually. The city also has several fine theater companies.

Surprisingly, one great city has been built among the coastal mountains. San Francisco was founded as a small mission and fort at the base of the mountains, but when California's economy began to boom so did San Francisco. The streets and houses climb right up the mountain-sides. The hills are so sheer it is no wonder that San Francisco invented a special form of transportation to get over them. The cable cars which are pulled up the steep hills are as much fun as a roller-coaster ride, the way they hang out precariously over airy nothingness.

The hills also provide many fine scenic points. Places like Lafayette Park, which in any other city would be just a nice patch of greenery, stick in the memory because of the hilltop views they provide. The Golden Gate Bridge also gains much from its setting. It is a lovely bridge, but the feature that sets the Golden Gate apart from other suspension bridges is the wildness of its setting. It spans an ocean strait guarded by

The Pacific West

Seattle is nestled directly at the feet of the Cascade Mountains, a giant series of peaks and volcanic cones containing as many national parks as the Rockies. The greatest mountain in the chain is Rainier, a dormant volcano whose glacier-covered dome is easily seen from the ferries that cross Puget Sound. It stands 14,410 ft (4,392 m) tall and is a great place for hikers. Treks up to a glacier and back are easily made in a single day. Longer hikes, requiring several days, circumnavigate the base of the mountain along a trail that leads through enormous cedar forests and alpine meadows. The mountain receives a lot of snow and over the past 30 years many of the glaciers have grown considerably. During the winter of 1971–2 Mt Rainier experienced 93.5 ft (28.5 m) of snow, a world record.

While Rainier is the tallest of the mountains, the Cascades have other great peaks as well. Mt Hood (11,245 ft; 3,427 m) overlooks the Willamette Valley; Mt Shasta (14,162 ft; 4,317 m) stands at the top of the Sacramento Valley. All three mountains are popular with climbers. At one time a fourth, Mt Mazama, was another giant volcanic cone, but the walls collapsed and formed a crater which flooded and is now protected as Crater Lake National Park in southern Oregon. From the height of the rim the lake far below is a perfect mirror of the sky and shines with the profoundest blue color. The lake is extremely deep, 1,932 ft (589 m).

Despite the presence of all these volcanos, eruptions are rare. The only mountain in the group to erupt during historic times was Lassen, east of Redding in the Sacramento Valley. During the years 1914–7 Mt Lassen saw a series of eruptions which climaxed on 22 May 1915 when the mountain seemed to explode, sending a mushroom cloud 4 miles (6.5 km) into the sky. Ashes fell on Reno, Nevada, more than 100 miles (160 km) from the eruption.

The only natural route which leads beyond the Cascades is along the Columbia River. Plenty of rivers in the world are longer than the Columbia, but few cut through so mighty a chain of mountains. At one time the Columbia River Gorge was one of the outstanding sights of the north-west. Now, however, it has been dammed repeatedly and most of the gorge is lost to view. The first dam up the river is the Bonneville, located below Mt Hood. The dam itself is fairly impressive. The most interesting feature is the salmon ladder which permits migrating fish to climb up and over the dam. Greatest of all the Columbia River dams is the Grand Coulee in northern Washington. No dam in the world generates more electric power than this one. It has also been used to irrigate the interior Columbia plateau. Because of the Cascades, few clouds make it to eastern Washington and Oregon. The region is a natural desert, but more and more of it is now irrigated and planted.

The desert plateau quickly gives way to some of the most remote mountains and gorges in the old 48 states. It is also top-rank scenic country. A large part of it is reached by the Snake River which begins in Wyoming at the Continental Divide, digs its way through Idaho, and at last joins the Columbia River at Pasco, Washington. The Snake provides 40 per cent of the Columbia waters which reach the Pacific. These days much of the Snake is dammed too, but there are still lots of awesome views along its banks. The lower half of Hells Canyon on the Idaho-Oregon border is still wild. The canyon is the deepest gorge in North America, half a mile deeper than the Grand Canyon, though not so remarkably colored. Seven peaks, known as the Seven Devils, stand on the Idaho side looking down. Except for some Basque sheepherders the area

Above: Big Sur, California has become a popular resort and artists' colony. Such rugged beauty is dangerous to shipping and explains why inland bays are so important to Pacific trade.

Above right: The symmetrical massiveness of the ice-capped dome on Mt Shasta, California is typical of the volcanos found along the Cascade Range.

Right: Crater Lake National Park, Oregon is a collapsed volcano, or caldera. The crater's diameter is about 6 miles (9.6 km) and before the caldera was formed Mt Mazama probably reached 12,000 ft (3,600 m). Wizard Island was created by volcanic activity which occurred after the mountain collapsed. The lake's extraordinary color results from its great depth.

is still unoccupied by people and the canyon is good wildlife country. Mountain lions, elk, black bear, and mountain goat all live there. Further upriver, around Swan Falls, is a Birds of Prey Area with bald eagles, peregrine falcons, golden eagles, and the largest known breeding population of prairie falcons.

It was quite a feat for the Snake to have found a path through Idaho. The state has 81 named mountain ranges and over half of the land is 5,000–10,000 ft (1,500–3,000 m) high. Slowly the reputation of the Idaho mountains has begun to spread. The Sawtooth Mountains in the south have become a busy summer place, and the tiny town of Stanley, with a year-round population of 47, now has 12,000 people in the summer. Not far away is Sun Valley, America's oldest ski resort. The state is still big and rumpled enough, however, for an outdoorsman to find lots of seldom-walked trails, and of course the regular hunters and campers don't talk about their secret places—a hideaway along the Lochsa River, a trail through the Bitterroot Mountains, or a spot along the Salmon River (also called 'The River of No Return') where cutthroat trout come to spawn. There is not much country anywhere in the States that is finer than Idaho.

The Desert

The Desert

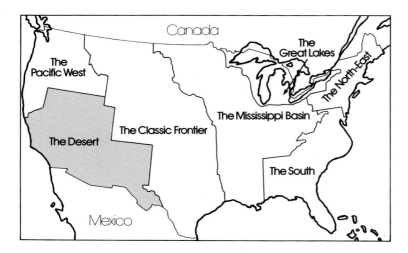

The Spanish conquistadors were practical men who went to the ends of the earth hoping to find riches, not natural beauty. So in 1540 Lopéz de Cárdenas felt justified in telling Coronado, his commanding officer, that the Grand Canyon was 'a useless piece of country.'

Three centuries later explorers came to the area once again. John Wesley Powell led a journey down the Colorado River in 1869 and at the entrance to the Grand Canyon made this comment in his diary: 'We are three-quarters of a mile in the depths of the earth and the great river shrinks into insignificance as it dashes its angry waves against the walls and cliffs that rise to the world above; they are but puny ripples and we but pigmies running up and down the sand or lost among the boulders.'

Although their tones were quite different, the two men were both taking note of the same fact. People do not have much effect on the Grand Canyon. Even today the trails tramped by millions of people every year are no more than hairlines across an enormous sea of scraped and carved rocks. The canyon swallows mountains whole; how can it be expected to do other than make the ambitions and capacities of people seem small?

From Hopi Point, the popular viewing spot on the south rim, one can sit and look down on colors, mountains, and ravines spread out for miles. Off to the left is a huge natural amphitheater. If it were anywhere else, it would be world-famous for its wildness, size, and sheer walls. But in the Grand Canyon the amphitheater is just one more dazzling speck of detail in an abundant canvas. The beauty of the place comes from this rich expansiveness; it is as humbling as the starry sky.

The Grand Canyon is the greatest sight in the collection of deserts and semi-deserts that spread west from the Pecos River in Texas to the California coast and even beyond. Coastal islands like Santa Catalina are deserts too.

Two of the desert sections spill over from Mexico. The Chihuahua Desert extends into west Texas, while the Sonora crosses into California and Arizona. The Texas desert scenery is chiefly mountainous. The Chisos Mountains in Big Bend National Park include some fairly easy hiking trails to good viewpoints. The Guadalupe Mountains, with a national park of their own, are more demanding. In California the Imperial Valley portion of the Sonora Desert is now heavily irrigated and productive farmland. The brackish Salton Sea in the valley is the result of this irrigation; the lake only appeared early in this century.

The region strongest in scenic beauty is the Colorado Plateau of northern Arizona and New Mexico and most of

Previous pages: From Zabriskie Point, Death Valley is a land of frightening emptiness. Today it is the driest and hottest place in North America.

Left: Grand Canyon National Park, Arizona encompasses the deepest and most spectacular portion of the desert gorge.

Below left: Colorful sand and limestone formations

fill Bryce Canyon National Park, Utah.

Below: Hoover Dam sits on the Arizona-Nevada border blocking the Black Canyon of the Colorado River.

Bottom: California's Imperial Valley is naturally a desert; one almost as ferocious as Death Valley. Irrigation has made it an agricultural center which is particularly important for its winter crop.

Utah. It is not quite as dry as neighboring territories and has deep canyons. Besides the Grand Canyon there are Bryce, Zion, and the gorges of Canyonlands National Park. The soils are more colorful too, reaching their wildest display east of the Grand Canyon in the Painted Desert. The mineral stains on the earth are called 'desert varnish.'

Running through the desert like the Nile is the Colorado River, now a major source of irrigation. The two greatest dams on the river are Hoover Dam (formerly called Boulder Dam) and Glen Canyon Dam. Since the construction of these dams involved the flooding of several impressive canyons they are

Above left: Sand dunes in Death Valley National Monument.

Above: The Cliff Palace in Mesa Verde National Park, Colorado contains hundreds of rooms and is the largest of the many such structures, or pueblos, in the mesa. These dwellings were probably abandoned because of a prolonged drought lasting from 1277–99 and then Navajo and Apache migrations may have prevented the people's return.

Above right: Cactus in Saguaro National Monument, Arizona can live for 200 years.

Far left: Boat trips down the Colorado River are an outdoorsman's dream.

Left: San Xavier del Bac, the White Dove of the Desert, was built in 1797 by Franciscans near modern Tucson, Arizona.

rather controversial. Defenders of the projects insist that the opening of new land to farming and settlement has been worth the loss of scenic splendor.

A journey up California's eastern side finds lots of desert types. The most famous and most arid portion is Death Valley, named by some unfortunate pioneers who crossed it in 1849. The heat in the valley is terrible. The hottest ever recorded air temperature there was 134°F (57°C) while ground temperatures can reach 190°F (88°C). Shimmering in the haze on the valley's western side are the Panamint Mountains, rising almost 2 miles (3 km) above the desert floor; they tempted early travelers by looking so close, but the anvil of heat that lay between gave the valley its name.

While Death Valley has a number of fresh-water springs and even a river, the best place to see a desert oasis is a bit south at Joshua Tree National Monument. Springs enclosed by palm trees are in marked contrast to the desert surroundings. Some wildlife can also be found there – lizards, bobcats, coyotes, and bighorn sheep.

The Panamints are part of a series of north–south mountains in this area known as the Basin Ranges, semi-arid mountains that rise between desert valleys. The outstanding ones are the Sierra Nevada, a California extension of the Cascades of the north-west. The highest peak in the range (and in the old 48 states) is Mt Whitney, 14,494 ft (4,418 m).

The slopes of the Sierra Nevada are forested, even containing giant sequoia trees. Yosemite National Park, King's Canyon National Park, and Sequoia National Park are all in the Sierra Nevada and serve as scenic marvels of forest, rock, and waterfalls in the midst of otherwise dry land. Much of the water in southern California is run off from the Sierra Nevada.

Survival in this region depends absolutely on the prudent control of water. Ancient Indian cliff dwellings were appar-

Below left: In 1827 Joseph Smith announced that an angel had revealed the 'Book of Mormon' to him. Smith's preaching brought persecution and in 1844 he was murdered, but his surviving disciples, led by

Brigham Young, found safety in the Utah desert. Although the setting was not promising, Mormon doctrine emphasizes progress and human potential. The great temple in Salt Lake City was built

in 1892 and testifies eloquently to the Mormon success in Utah.

Below: Sun City, Arizona pioneered in developing real estate projects where homes are sold only to the elderly.

ently abandoned when the drought grew too severe. In southern Arizona, near Organ Pipe Cactus National Monument, irrigation ditches were constructed by the Indians of long ago and some are now being used again by modern settlers.

New water projects have made the southern desert the busiest frontier in America. It is the place where unoccupied land is being settled and developed at the greatest pace. Every desert city can trace its rise to some particular water-control system. Phoenix, Arizona began to expand after the construction of the Theodore Roosevelt Dam on the Salt River. Las Vegas, Nevada would never have become a gambling resort if it were not for the Hoover Dam.

The Mormons are the pioneer group with the oldest success at building cities in the desert. They fled into the Utah wilderness in 1847 and were able to establish a system of irrigation good enough to support farms and towns. Salt Lake City, Utah's capital, is not so much beautiful as it is interesting. The Mormon Temple and Tabernacle are the most remarkable buildings in the state and serve as the center of the faith which brought the first pioneers to the area. Like the Pilgrims, the Quakers, and the Pennsylvania Dutch, Utah's Mormons were hoping to establish a community where they could be left to themselves. They found an added advantage in the fact that they had few rivals for their desert territory. They never were overwhelmed by outsiders and Utah today is still more than two-thirds Mormon.

The greatest of America's desert cities is Los Angeles. Stories of how the city got control over so much of southern California's scarce water tell of secrecy, ambition, and daring. The result has been remarkable. The nation's third largest city stands in a desert. Almost 90 per cent of its water is piped in from the Owens Valley east of the Sierra Nevada, or from the Colorado River, or even from northern California. The aqueducts and reservoirs provide enough water to support grassy lawns, great flower gardens, and swimming pools in many a backyard.

Los Angeles is built in a flatland surrounded on three sides by low mountains–the ocean is on the fourth side. Because of its heat, its people, and its cars, the basin is often filled with a hazy smog, but on clear days sharp mountain walls leap into view and remind everyone that they are living in a place of great natural beauty.

There are plenty of man-made attractions as well. The suburb of Anaheim was the birthplace of theme parks, and Disneyland draws millions of visitors per year–on a summer weekend it can seem like millions per day. The movie and television industries draw people from all over the world, though there is little to see. Travelers wind up taking tours to see the high walls that guard the homes of movie stars, but at the conclusion of the tour they find an unexpected reward. Having climbed high into the Santa Monica mountains and found little to photograph, they turn to descend. Suddenly the whole of the Los Angeles basin is below them. Far to the south are other mountains and in between, for mile after mile, is the city with its houses, streets, and freeways. It is not at all what people expect to find in a desert.

Below: Los Angeles' many private swimming pools demonstrate the city's success at bringing water into the desert.

Bottom left: Los Angeles' greatest growth was during the 1950s and 60s when faith in the automobile was at its peak. Its freeway system is unrivaled.

Bottom right: The casinos of Las Vegas, Nevada are active 24 hours a day.

Beyond the West

Beyond the West

Alaska's islands extend both east and west. The eastern ones form the state's panhandle, which has dense forests and a climate much like the Oregon and Washington coast. The panhandle also contains the state's oldest cities, Sitka and Juneau, which date back to the old fur-trapping days. But the islands and towns of the panhandle are isolated and remote, accessible only by ferry or plane and now the center of Alaskan activities has shifted elsewhere.

The western Aleutian Islands stretch out so far they cross the 180th meridian and enter the eastern hemisphere. These islands, too, seem small and distant. Often buried in banks of cold fog, they hold little promise of an active future. It is the massive bulk of central Alaska that points toward tomorrow.

Half of the state's 400,000 people live in or near the city of Anchorage, on the southern flank of central Alaska. The city was largely rebuilt after the 1964 earthquake; however, it is the scenery of Alaska which is the state's wonder and appeal. Little rivalry has come from its architects. The Chugach Mountains rise behind Anchorage to provide an amphitheater of broad ridges and to hint at the great rocky beauty of the state's interior.

Two major mountain systems cross Alaska. The southern one, the Alaska Range, contains Mt McKinley (known locally as Denali), the highest peak in North America. About two-thirds of its 20,300 ft (6,190 m) rises above the surrounding country, making the Alaska Range one of the most dramatic natural walls on earth. Like Zeus of old, Mt McKinley is a cloud-gatherer and its summit is usually hidden behind mists. Visitors can wait days or even weeks in order to snap a photo that shows the top of McKinley.

North of the mountains is the Alaska people commonly think of when they imagine the place. The land is mostly tundra, mainly uninhabited, and usually cold. Alaskans don't like people to talk about the state's cold, but they are fighting a losing battle because it *is* cold. The parts north of the Alaska Range are sometimes killingly frigid. The town of Tanana, at the junction of the Yukon and Tanana Rivers, holds the all-time low temperature record for the state, −76°F (−60°C). That temperature plus a fearsome wind has kept the population of the Yukon Valley low.

The Yukon Valley is one of the last great wildernesses on earth. It is a place of migrating caribou, of free-ranging bears, and of hunting wolf packs. No place in America can equal it for wildlife, for unexplored hiking country, or for its simple vastness. A summer expedition into the area is the ambition, or at least the fantasy, of most of the outdoorsmen in America.

The caribou, or reindeer, of the Alaskan interior make an annual migration up to the Arctic shore. To do so they must cross Alaska's northern mountains, the Brooks Range. These are much lower than the southern peaks, the highest being Mt Isto's 9,058 ft (2,760 m). Many of the range's western summits are below 5,000 ft (1,500 m). The mountains are cold and barren, however, for they lie entirely within the Arctic Circle and are above the timber line.

It is north of the Brooks Range that the practical men of the world have now turned their eyes. In terms of precipitation this area is a desert, getting as little rain or snow as Yuma, Arizona or Las Vegas, Nevada. The temperatures are not as fierce as in the interior, but it is still plenty cold and the wind is terrifying. Until the late 1960s the area was left almost exclusively to the Eskimos. Barrow, at the state's northern tip, was the world's largest Eskimo town. It lies within 1,300 miles (2,090 km) of the North Pole. Then, in 1968, an oil-field as rich as that of Texas was discovered on this north slope of the Brooks Range.

The oil discovery brought the question of Alaska's future to a head. Should it be mined and exploited for short-term gains the way it was during a former gold rush? Or should it be treated as a treasure-chest of long-term beauty? The questions are still provoking bitter disputes and the answer to the problem is not yet clear.

Previous pages: The snowfields which sit on the top half of Mt McKinley feed into glaciers which can be 30 miles (48 km) long.

Top: Sitka was founded in 1804 as the capital of Russian America, as Alaska was known before its purchase by the US

Government in 1867. Today
it is a small fishing town.

Above: Alaska's original
inhabitants were the

Eskimos and they are still
the state's most important
minority. They have always
lived by hunting and great
catches of fish are preserved

by drying (left). Their
clothing always used to be
very carefully hand-tailored
to fit the individual;
however, these days when

they gather to enjoy a
festivity some Eskimos can
be seen wearing a modern
non-traditional zipper
(right).

Left: Waikiki Beach is one of the world's most popular vacation spots. Even in the days before tourists began coming to the island in their thousands, the beach was the special resort of Hawaiian royalty.

In land-hungry Hawaii such debates are over. The issue has been settled in favor of extensive development. Cities, suburbs, and farms are major parts of most of the island views. Even the crater floor of Diamond Head Mountain now has buildings in it. In fact, land pressures are so great that the famous pineapple and sugar-cane industries are beginning to shrink as farmland is gradually converted into residential or resort property.

These pressures are strongest on the island of Oahu, third largest in the chain of 132 islands in the Hawaiian archipelago. Eighty per cent of Hawaii's population lives there, over half of them on the southern rim around Honolulu, the state capital. Oahu is also the principal goal for the many travelers who come to Hawaii in search of warm waters and hot, sunny beaches.

Just east of Honolulu is Waikiki Beach, one of the most popular resort spots on earth. Most of the hotel buildings are new and built in the modern style, tall and dull, but they provide 21,000 rooms. The queen of the beach is the famous old Royal Hawaiian Hotel, a massive pink flamboyance with a cupola more typical of Renaissance Rome than of Polynesia. Its design is so extravagant that just looking at the hotel is fun. Guarding the end of the beach is Diamond Head, a gracefully sloped extinct volcano that stands 760 ft (230 m) tall.

Oahu is also the chief island for people who go to beaches to surf rather than to get a tan or merely splash about. Sunset Beach, on Oahu's north side, is one of the great surfing points of the world. Waves five times the size of the surfers give rides that, for the really brave and skilled, can last up to a minute.

With such a concentration of people on Oahu, the other islands make good destinations for travelers interested in avoiding crowds. Six other islands in the group are inhabited. They are Hawaii, Maui, Kauai, Niihau, Lanai, and Molokai. Each of these islands was built by a volcanic upheaval and each is characterized by a central mountain or mountain-group that slopes down to the beaches. Haena Beach on Kauai

Below: Kilauea is the largest active volcanic mass in the world.

Bottom: Hawaii's Polynesian people arrived in two waves. The first came from the Marquesas around

AD 400. The second, from Tahiti, arrived around AD 1000.

Below: Pearl Harbor sits behind Honolulu. Its many anchorages and lochs have made it the center of the navy's Pacific command.

is the one that looks the way everyone knows a Pacific island beach should look; it has appeared in many movies, including *South Pacific*.

While Hawaii's beaches draw the visitors, the volcanic craters are worth exploring too. Wildest of all is Haleakala Crater on Maui. Sinking half a mile below the mountain peak, the crater looks the way the moon must be. It is a sterile land marked by conical hills of lava cinders.

The largest island, Hawaii, still has active volcanos and offers the best chance in America of seeing an eruption. The eastern craters are the most active, with Kilauea being the most dramatic during recent years. The island is the tallest mountain mass on earth. It rises almost 19,680 ft (6,000 m) from the floor of the Pacific before even reaching the ocean surface and then stands another 13,680 ft (4,170 m) above sea level. The total height of the largest mountain, Mauna Kea, is 33,476 ft (10,203 m), four-fifths of a mile higher than Mount Everest. In winter Mauna Kea is covered in snow and is the

site of a ski festival.

Perhaps the greatest view on the islands is atop the Na Pali Cliffs on Kauai. The cliffs are ribbed, as though supported by gothic buttresses, and stand over 3,000 ft (900 m) high. Down below, ancient irrigation terraces built by the Polynesians can still be seen. Between the bases of the cliff buttresses are thick jungle patches of vegetation. The easiest way to reach the valley floor is still by sea and this remoteness accounts for its wild state.

Both the Hawaiian Islands and Alaska were of interest to the American government first for their strategic military location, but it is a mistake to suppose that they are mere appendages to the other 48 states. They too have built a new society which blends immigrant heritages with local conditions and the national system. Neither state is nearly as remote as Oregon and California were when they joined the Union. The special features of their tropic and arctic scenery enrich and complete the rest of the diverse beauty of America.